HOW TO CREATE INTEREST-EVOKING, SALES-INDUCING, NON-IRRITATING ADVERTISING
Walter Weir

SOME ADVANCE REVIEWS

"Executives concerned about the effectiveness of their advertising will keep this book within reach for excellent judging criteria, particularly the chapter on 'How to Analyze an Advertisement'. . . . Doctors have their PDR or Physicians Desk Reference; now advertising professionals have their ADR or Advertising Desk Reference. While written for professionals and students, consumers–the target of advertising–will find this interesting and informative non-fiction reading."

Thomas A. Mitchell, BA, MBA
Marketing/Advertising Consultant
Holland, PA

"Walter Weir's new book on advertising–with its full, descriptive, and accurate title–is impressively unique. Each step to good advertising is planned carefully and emanates from Weir's success in the worlds of advertising and higher education. For the student, the book is a godsend. For the professional, Weir has repaved the road to profitable advertising."

Frederic B. Farrar, MA
Professor Emeritus, Communications
Temple University

"A unique (and hitherto unimaginable) combination: the perfect textbook for the student of advertising and the perfect reference book for the practitioner. Its strength lies in the brilliance of its brevity. It is clear, concise, and easily understood. One emerges from it a far better judge of advertising and a far better craftsman."

Anthony Weir
Managing Director, Whitford Corporation
Former Regional Managing Director
Ogilvy & Mather and Leo Burnett

"In 42 easily accessible chapters, this important figure of modern advertising tells all those wishing to learn how to think about advertising and how to create it—for the benefit of the client, the writer, and, not incidently, the readers/viewers/listeners of those messages."

Kim B. Rotzoll, PhD
Professor and Head of the Department of Advertising
University of Illinois at Urbana-Champaign

How to Create Interest-Evoking, Sales-Inducing, Non-Irritating Advertising

HAWORTH Marketing Resources
Innovations in Practice & Professional Services
William J. Winston, Senior Editor

New, Recent, and Forthcoming Titles:

Long Term Care Administration: The Management of Institutional and Non-Institutional Components of the Continuum of Care by Ben Abramovice

Cases and Select Readings in Health Care Marketing, edited by Robert E. Sweeney, Robert L. Berl, and William J. Winston

Marketing Planning Guide by Robert E. Stevens, David L. Loudon, and William E. Warren

Marketing for Churches and Ministries by Robert E. Stevens and David L. Loudon

The Clinician's Guide to Managed Mental Health Care by Norman Winegar

Framework for Market-Based Hospital Pricing Decisions by Shahram Heshmat

Professional Services Marketing: Strategy and Tactics by F. G. Crane

A Guide to Preparing Cost-Effective Press Releases by Robert H. Loeffler

How to Create Interest-Evoking, Sales-Inducing, Non-Irritating Advertising by Walter Weir

Market Analysis: Assessing Your Business Opportunities by Robert E. Stevens, Philip K. Sherwood, and J. Paul Dunn

Marketing for Attorneys and Law Firms edited by William J. Winston

Selling Without Confrontation by Jack Greening

Persuasive Advertising for Entrepreneurs and Small Business Owners: How to Create More Effective Sales Messages by Jay P. Granat

Marketing Mental Health Services in a Managed Care Environment by Norman Winegar and John L. Bistline

How to Create Interest-Evoking, Sales-Inducing, Non-Irritating Advertising

Walter Weir

Fellow of the
American Academy of Advertising

The Haworth Press
New York • London • Norwood (Australia)

The Haworth Press, Inc., 10 Alice Street, Binghamton, NY 13904-1580

Library of Congress Cataloging-in-Publication Data

Weir, Walter,
    How to create interest-evoking, sales-inducing, non-irritating advertising / Walter Weir.
        p.   cm
    Includes bibliographical references and index.
    ISBN 1-56024-238-8 (acid free paper).
    1. Advertising copy. 2. Advertising – Management. I. Title.
HF5825.W397   1992
659.1 – dc20
                                                                        91-34585
                                                                        CIP

CONTENTS

Other Works by Author

On the Writing of Advertising
Truth in Advertising and Other Heresies
Meager Music – Collected Poems

ABOUT THE AUTHOR

Walter Weir, a corporate, marketing, and advertising communications consultant, has over sixty years experience in the advertising field. For eight years he taught advertising — at Michigan State, the University of Tennessee, and Temple University. Mr. Weir has lectured extensively on advertising and written profusely for the trade press. For twenty-five years, he anonymously wrote "Creative Man's Corner," a readers' favorite in *Advertising Age*. He is the author of several books, including the widely used *On the Writing of Advertising* (McGraw-Hill, 1961). Mr. Weir has worked with the governments of Puerto Rico and Israel to help with special marketing problems, and during World War II worked with then Secretary of the Treasury Morgenthau on a campaign to help overcome the United States' apathy toward the War. In March of 1992 Weir was made a Fellow of the American Academy of Advertising for his contributions to advertising education.

Foreword

The publication of this kind of book is long overdue. It is authoritative not only by virtue of the author's long successful experience as a master copywriter, but also because he has been a planner, manager, entrepreneur, and top agency executive. It also contains the wisdom of one who has taught his subject at three universities, in particular, Temple University where this book was developed and tested.

This book is brilliantly concise but still comprehensive. The author reduces complex ideas to a brief, easy-to-understand form. Often he says more in a few words than other authors say in several paragraphs.

As one of its foremost practitioners, Walter Weir has also been one of advertising's severest critics. For more than 25 years he was the anonymous author of "Creative Man's Corner" in *Advertising Age*. Recently he was unmasked, and prepared an article for *Advertising Age* entitled: "The Secret Life of an Advertising Critic." He wrote: "During the years I wrote 'The Corner,' several times I saw fit to criticize advertising from my own agency, including advertising I had written. This wasn't difficult because there isn't a piece of copy that I have written that I would not rewrite if it were going to be rerun. My attitude is that good copy is not written; it's rewritten. Many times." He added that he was "critical of copy written with insufficient research, thought, discipline, or clarity." These words explain a great deal about this book.

My years as an educator have taught me that students need a method to learn how to do acceptable and successful advertising. It is not enough to provide theory or examples of past advertising. This book provides such a method. It avoids the error of presenting numerous examples of past advertising as if they were suitable to guide future advertising. There is not a single glossy print ad in the book. Instead, Walter Weir describes his examples in words and explains why they were or were not successful. He demonstrates by showing readers how to think clearly. The main task of the teacher is to impart this reasoning process to students. They can then develop their individual styles to produce advertising that will be acceptable and successful under future conditions. Therefore, this book should be welcomed by those who teach advertising.

Each chapter is only a few pages long. The technique is to divide material into short teachable segments while following a logical development of ideas. Each chapter contains thought-provoking discussion questions and an assignment that requires the student to do one or more of the following: (1) seek out examples of particular kinds of advertising (a very practical habit), (2) do an advertisement, or (3) do a short project. The number of chapters corresponds to the number of hours in a one-semester three-credit course.

Based on a lifetime of experience, this book is nevertheless thoroughly in harmony with a modern understanding of marketing, consumer behavior, and advertising as a business and social institution. It contains a practical, step-by-step, developmental collection of topics that explain how to plan, write, and design successful advertising that is also socially acceptable. If more advertising writers used Walter Weir's methods there would be far fewer criticisms of advertising and less need for government regulation.

I have read a large number of advertising textbooks over the years, but never have I read one that makes me feel so confident that the book will be uniquely successful in helping young people to learn how to do successful advertising. After reading this book I know why former Weir students speak so highly of him.

Finally, although this superbly written book is designed for students, it will also be useful to account executives and other managers, including CEOs of large companies who need to evaluate the advertising they are asked to approve.

Gordon E. Miracle
Michigan State University

Introduction:
About this Book and How to Use It

This is a book intended for you to read and constantly refer to while you are analyzing, re-writing, and improving *current* advertising. It is a book based on the premise that 99 percent of advertising published and aired today can be improved.

Opinion surveys, for example, reveal that up to 75 percent of the adult public considers most advertising an "insult" to its intelligence. It is also common knowledge that television sets are equipped with "zappers" — not only to enable viewers to switch channels from where they are sitting and viewing but to push the mute button when television commercials interrupt the programs they are watching.

The book has been given the title, *How to Create Interest-Evoking, Sales-Inducing, Non-Irritating Advertising*. The initial chapters should be read in order to understand the basic nature of advertising as a human practice, as well as a business practice, and to have the constant awareness that advertising cannot be successful through the use of statements that promise more than the product can deliver. The chapters that follow relate ways in which an advertising message can most readily interest the logical prospects for the product or service and help them in deciding which product brands are most likely to bring them value and satisfaction in use, and give them reason for preferring and continuing to purchase such brands.

You will find no examples of advertisements that have been declared at one time or another to have been outstanding or to have won awards. They may illustrate the kind of originality of design and of word choice that caused them to be outstanding at one time. They are not to be looked upon as patterns to be faithfully copied for similar results today, for the circumstances under which they appeared no longer exist. The illustrative device — the black eye-patch — that caused *The Man in the Hathaway Shirt* to obtain so much notice would not be as likely to attract so much attention if used in an advertisement for another product — such as *The Man in the Aquascutum Raincoat.* Even the original Hathaway advertisement might not be as effective if repeated. As evidence of the effect of changing circumstances on advertising, the famous Volkswagen campaign that caused the Beetle to become the largest selling imported automobile was incapable, despite its continuing originality and brilliance, to maintain that position for Volkswagen when Japanese imports — notably the Toyota and the Datsun — appeared, neither of which was introduced with advertising one-quarter as distinctive or unique as the Volkswagen advertising.

The daily need in advertising is considerably less for outstanding or memorable advertisements or commercials than it is for *messages interesting enough to invite inspection and reading and sufficiently clear, factual, and persuasive to induce inspection and purchase of the product.* This is by no means intended to imply that an advertisement should be written or designed with any less care and devotion than any other literary undertaking. Dedication to excellence in communication is essential to the ultimate effectiveness of any advertising message.

In this respect, the reading of any text cannot produce competence in the subject of which it treats. We learn best and become competent quickest by *doing.* Consequently, this text is chaptered so that, after the fundamental nature of commercial persuasion is grasped and understood, the reader can analyze current advertising messages to determine what may be lacking for evoking interest in what is being advertised.

As a consequence, the name of the product can be noted and a letter written to the advertiser asking for the script of the particular commercial heard or seen. To obtain the address of the advertiser, ask for the Standard Directory of Advertisers at the public library which lists the names, officers, and addresses of most major advertisers. This directory is called by professionals "the Red Book" because of its red cover. Under each advertiser is also listed the name of the advertising agency (or agencies) responsible for the company's advertising. The agency's address and officers, together with the accounts it handles, can be found in the Standard Directory of Advertising Agencies. If the public library does not have these directories, it is possible that a local advertising agency may have them. Address your letter to the president of the company or of the advertising agency or the company's advertising manager. Explain your reason for asking for the script — you are studying advertising and wish to have a script of the commercial you saw.

If you have a voice tape, of course, and have it at hand — even *in* hand — as you are watching a TV show or listening to the radio, you can record at least the audio part of the TV commercial, which may help you remember the video.

You can also write down your reaction to the commercial and why you either liked it or disliked it — then, if you disliked it, re-do it as you think it should have been done and ask friends or family members or fellow students their appraisal of what you have done. If you have a VCR, you can record a program together with its commercials and analyze the latter, re-doing them as your analysis and current knowledge of advertising cause you to think they should be done.

As is said elsewhere in this book, the best way to learn is by doing, not once but several times, and not just once in a while but every day, until your work reflects the fact that you have learned how advertising messages should be done to evoke interest, induce sales, and not be irritating to read, hear, or see.

Chapter 1

Understanding Advertising

If you plan to write advertising or plan to be in a position in which you may have to judge it (as an account executive with an advertising agency or as an advertising director or a product manager with a company that advertises), you will function more effectively if you have a thorough awareness and understanding of the nature, the background, the scope, and the current state of the craft.

Advertising is communication employed on a large scale essentially to persuade. The purpose of the persuasion is generally to bring about the desired aim of an individual, a corporation, an association, or a political party. The individual may need employment and, to that end, run a job-wanted advertisement in the classified advertising section of a newspaper. A corporation may want to induce a number of consumers about to buy a motor car to consider the purchase of a particular model and, for that purpose, run a national advertising campaign in selected newspapers in, say, the top 100 markets of the country. The association may want to increase the use of oranges or potatoes grown by its members and, to accomplish this, establish a brand name by which the oranges or the potatoes can be identified and asked for and promote the advantages of buying oranges or potatoes identified by that name (or brand) by running an advertising campaign in the women's service magazines. A candidate for political office may wish to campaign for that office with the aid of messages on radio or on television promoting a particular qualification. Whatever the aim, the advertising published or broadcast to achieve it usually cites (1) the benefits to be obtained by responding positively to the message; (2) the singular capacity to provide those benefits of whatever is mentioned in the advertising; and (3) supporting evidence attesting to this capacity.

The degree of positive response is generally in direct proportion to the degree of conviction or favorable attitude of mind obtained among those exposed to the message. This conviction or attitude, in turn, is affected and conditioned by the facts presented and the manner of their presentation. The selection and manner of presentation of the facts are invariably affected by the training, the experience, the skill, and — most vital of all — *the particular philosophy* of the writer of the message. These more than anything else that goes into the message most directly affect the reaction of the individuals who read or hear it. It is to the proper cultivation and effective employment of these vital factors that this volume is addressed.

As employed commercially to stimulate the purchase and use of products and services, advertising is necessarily a phase of marketing. It is used to help achieve the marketing goal through effective communication with the individuals comprising the market. Marketing includes the planning by which products or services come into being and are made available for purchase. It is the process through which such products are invested with qualities that will make them most likely to be purchased — their particular features, the price at which they will be offered, how they will be packaged, where and how they will be offered for sale. Too many products and services are "launched" with little or no market planning and, when this occurs, the manufacturer generally employs advertising to suggest plausible reasons for purchase. It is possible for advertising to create a favorable impression of a product but not to invest it with qualities it lacks. Ultimately there is a "moment of truth" when the purchaser uses the product. If the purchaser has been led by the advertising to expect more than the product provides, he or she either returns the product to the manufacturer or never buys it again. In addition, the purchaser can be expected to spread word of its deficiencies.

Advertising is a major activity with annual expenditures in the billions of dollars. The cost of advertising is inescapably included in the price of the product. However, that cost is usually countable in pennies, even fractions of a penny. No less expensive way to stimulate sales has been evolved or discovered. The most expensive, though frequently the most effective way, is personal contact which can cost hundreds of dollars a call.

The primary contribution of advertising is creating confidence in products, services, or individuals by making them *familiar* over a period of time. The public appears to conclude that such products, services, or people must be reliable or they would not still be on the market place.

It is to be wondered why so major a force as advertising should also be one of the most criticized of commercial practices. If you plan to write advertising, you should acquaint yourself with the attitude towards advertising of the people you will be addressing. You should learn firsthand the amount of annoyance, irritation, skepticism, and even disbelief your messages will encounter, and which, unless you are aware of, they may enhance. You should know that some advertisers not only find this totally acceptable but frequently look upon it as evidence of the impact and effectiveness of their advertising. Unfortunately advertising that irritates and an-noys does occasionally prove effective — more effective than adver-tising so bland as to make no impression at all. At the same time, a review of successful advertising over the years will reveal that most of it in no way, to use a common phrase, "insulted the intelli-gence" of the public, while a review of advertising that *was* consid-ered to insult the intelligence will reveal it to have been so consid-ered chiefly because of incompetence in its preparation. It is the purpose of this volume to enable you to create advertising that is effectively persuasive yet acceptable and even welcomed by those to whom it is addressed.

QUESTIONS, SUBJECTS FOR DISCUSSION

1. In what way can an account executive, an advertising director, or a brand manager benefit from knowing what is required for the writing of effective, non-irritating advertising?

2. What is the general purpose of advertising?

3. What is generally needed to cause a consumer to respond posi-tively to an advertising message?

4. What are the two most vital factors in creating an effective advertising message?

5. Why is advertising so widely used, both nationally and on the local level?

6. What are some of the criticisms made of advertising? Why is it useful for a copywriter to be aware of these?

PROJECT

Interview a minimum of twenty adults and ask them their opinion of and attitude toward advertising. What do they think of it? Do they find it reliable? If they were going to buy a car, for example, would they consider themselves sufficiently informed to make a wise purchase simply by reading the advertising of cars within their price bracket? If not, what other sources of information would they consult — and why?

Do they think advertising tells the whole story? If not, what would they consider the whole story? Do they feel advertisers occasionally stoop to deception — or to exaggeration? What do they feel can be done to avoid this? What kind of advertising do they like best? In what way or ways can advertising cause them to believe that what it tells them about a product or a service is truthful?

Do they find advertising helpful or annoying — or both? What kind of advertising do they find helpful? Why? What kind of advertising do they find annoying or irritating — and why? What do they think could be done to make advertising non-irritating? What is their opinion of people in advertising?

Do not limit yourself to the questions covered here. Do attempt to obtain candid opinions.

Chapter 2

A Human Practice

Textbooks introducing students to advertising generally trace its origins to early notices soliciting help in locating and returning runaway slaves and offering a reward as an incentive. They attribute the birth of modern advertising to the industrial revolution, the capacity of machines to bring about a greater output of product than could be sold within the manufacturer's locale and the consequent need to make the product known more widely, and thus, to stimulate sales of it through retailers stocking it for purchase. (Advertising is frequently employed to create a demand for a product sufficiently compelling to *cause* retailers to stock it, and display it, and even mention it in their own advertising.)

With so simplistic an explanation of advertising it can be understood why it is looked upon as primarily a business-brought-about activity. The conception of advertising as a purely commercial practice is bolstered further by daily observation of the use of it by business organizations from local retail shops to manufacturers of products distributed nationally and internationally. And — considering the dollar volume of advertising — there can be little doubt that advertising does appear to be essentially a business activity. However, advertising, as a persuasive factor in human intercourse, has "been around" since human beings first put in their appearance, or, at least, was first instituted when human beings attempted to live together. The establishment of *individual identity* became necessary because individuals assume or are given particular duties and must have some means of being singled out as the performer of such duties. Countless surnames came into being precisely in this way — Smith, Carpenter, Taylor — and once identity was established, the factor of competition manifested itself. Individuals vied with one another for recognition, acceptance, and preference.

What occurred in pre-literate times among human beings persists today. In childhood, individuals vie with one another, they compete for attention, love, favor, acclaim, position. To do this, they promote themselves; they resort to self-advertising, to their parents, their groups, their teachers, their schoolmates. Later in life they promote their desirability to potential employers. Needing a loan, they devise an "advertising campaign" directed at having an officer in a banking institution accept them as a desirable risk. The very people who criticize businesses for being "one-sided" in the advertising of their product, for confining what is printed or said about those products to the affirmative only, to what is favorable, carefully omitting what may be negative or unfavorable without thinking of their own manner of self-promotion, perform similarly. It is a sobering if not enlightening experience for everyone who condemns commercial advertising for being only "half" truthful, as well as occasionally "stretching" the truth, to reflect on how they have "advertised" themselves since early childhood. If they do they will also better understand why most people take advertising with the proverbial grain of salt—they will become aware of its purpose and of the manner in which it is phrased to achieve that purpose. They will be dissuaded from all too easily assuming that people are innocent and unaware of the artifices and devices of the professional persuader. They will also be conscious of the importance of truth and indisputable support for the claims made in advertising.

Because advertising is fundamentally a human practice that has been adopted by business, it can be understood why, in most universities, it is taught not in the School of Business Administration but in the Department of Journalism. For advertising is fundamentally *reporting*—the reporting of information about products and services and what they have to offer. Just as students majoring in journalism are taught to assemble all relevant facts about a fire, a murder, a robbery, an accident, so students majoring in advertising should be taught to assemble all relevant facts about whatever it is they are given to advertise and to report those facts in the advertising they write clearly, vividly, and accurately.

In this respect, a copywriting tyro should avoid the false assumption so many people make of advertising—that all it requires to be effective is a clever slogan or a number of highly imaginative phrases. The beginning advertiser must be constantly mindful that advertising must be factual, must be concrete, must be specific. The initial tendency of most students is to employ generalities, to use superlatives, to exaggerate, to make unfounded statements in the belief that people will be more likely to respond to puffery than to realistic description about what is being advertised. This is, of course, not so. People are no more likely to believe an advertisement that overstates and boasts than they are a human being who overstates and boasts. The student must realize that he or she is an advocate in every sense, just as a lawyer is an advocate and the case that that lawyer presents must be believed if the verdict obtained is to be favorable, and to be believed it must present evidence that is obviously not fabricated but based on fact.

QUESTIONS, SUBJECTS FOR DISCUSSION

1. What is the dictionary definition of advertising and what is the Latin root from which it derives?

2. Can human beings in Western societies justifiably, as well as practically, be considered "products" that must compete with other "products" for use and benefit?

3. Do human beings tend to "package" themselves in order to be identified as they wish, for one reason or another, to *be* identified?

4. How can the manner in which a company's advertising is written affect the way in which the company is judged?

5. How would you, as a reporter, go about gathering pertinent facts about a product and what kind of facts would you, as an advertising copywriter, look for?

PROJECT

Write an essay of at least 500 words covering the many ways in which you have "advertised" yourself since almost the beginning of your life. Cite specific examples as best as you can remember them and, if possible, give your reasons for doing what you did or saying what you did. Did what you did or said bring about what you wished it to? If it did not, why do you think it failed?

Were you totally truthful in the "advertising" you created about yourself? If you were not, why weren't you? Were you conscious of dressing in a particular way to impress people? Why did you think it would impress them? Where do you think you got the idea to do this?

If possible, do your essay chronologically, beginning with your very earliest attempts to induce your parents to act in a way you wanted them to act. Follow this with your experiences in trying to win the favor of your teacher or to be looked upon favorably by your schoolmates. If you ever sought employment, try to remember how you planned to "market" yourself. Did you provide references? If so, what did you think these references might be able to do to influence your prospective employer that *you* could not? In all instances in which you "advertised" yourself, why did you say what you did?

Chapter 3

The Importance of Writing Skill

In the writing of advertising, as in most human activities, incompetence prevails. It prevails primarily because few courses, beyond those required for the major, have to do with the acquiring of writing skill and literary competence. The only courses required in any way related to the development of writing skill are generally news writing and news editing; and the only requirement, usually, for students taking news writing and news editing is that they have passed English composition. *None of these requirements tends to inspire a student to excellence in expression or to acquaint that student with the art of creating interest in what he or she says.*

Yet, advertising demands as much writing skill and competence as the writing of short stories, plays, poetry, or essays. A news story generally has an inherent interest factor. It is generally about an exceptional or unusual happening. Advertising must be written for the most part about items with little inherent interest. It must create interest by relating these items, whatever they may be, to benefits that the reader, listener, or viewer will likely wish to have or enjoy. This requires much the same kind of "plotting" to create interest that a short story requires. The selection of words may not be as critical as in the writing of poetry, but the writer who has developed the discipline demanded by poetry will be more likely to choose more meaningful words than someone whose writing discipline has been no greater than that required for English composition. Similarly, the copywriter who writes a television commercial will write with considerably more interest and believability if that copywriter has acquired skill in character development and believable conversation from the study of playwriting. One of the most difficult kinds of advertising to invest with interest is so-called corporate advertising — advertising about a business intended to impart understanding of its policies or empathy with its management's point of view. The incisiveness, the illumination, the conviction of the well-written essay are invaluable for the writing of such advertising.

Generally recommended to the student of advertising are courses in the social sciences — political science, sociology, psychology; and these have their usefulness insofar as they acquaint the student with human behavior. But the need of the writer of advertising is not simply to know and understand human behavior but to be able to influence it through effective communication. It is useful to be familiar with human behavior and its motivations; it is vital to know how to convey in language the motivation that causes people to act. The price of a newspaper or a magazine page, for example, the cost of time on radio or television, are identical for all advertisers. But the results obtained from the space or the time vary; they vary in direct proportion to the *quality* of the communication. And that quality varies, of course, in direct proportion to the skill of the writer.

Unfortunately, an advertisement is seldom seen as an art form. In fact, copywriters are generally discouraged from ever considering advertising an art. They are encouraged, instead, to see advertising as a business procedure that is totally practical in purpose, in no way related to the writing of short stories or of novels or of plays which are generally seen as emanating from a fertile imagination rather than from a business-oriented mind. Yet no short story writer or novelist exists whose primary aim is not publication, as no playwright exists whose primary aim is not production, each an extremely practical and commercial goal. And the greater the artistic skill of the writer or the playwright, the more there will likely be commercial success. Because communication of any kind is fundamentally creative, it gains in intensity and in what it conveys from skills that are related to the arts rather than to business.

Copywriters should be acquainted with the nature of business and of business practice. They should be familiar with the various kinds of research on which they may have to call, with the essentials of marketing, product development, package design, distribution, pricing, and sales promotion — not only in order to understand the many other influences with which they will necessarily have to co-ordinate the advertising they create, but so that they can do so intelligently and effectively. But the contribution the copywriters make will be through the art of communication, and sheer business can teach them very little about this.

Give ten copywriters the same facts, the same research findings, and one of the ten will produce more successfully than the other nine. The difference is to some degree attributable to the kind and extent of the training undergone and to the kind and length of the experience acquired. However, above all, it is attributable to the quality of the communication and writing skill. Writing skill is compounded of many things, including the very intensity of the desire to do things well. It is compounded of what is absorbed from other writers, from what is learned of and from their style and, of course, from unrelenting writing. The copywriter who can let a single day go by without writing something, of whatever nature, is not likely to develop writing skill and should turn to some other, less demanding occupation.

QUESTIONS, SUBJECTS FOR DISCUSSION

1. Why is writing skill helpful to a writer of advertising?

2. Name primary advantages to be gained from the study of novel writing, short story writing, and the writing of poetry.

3. What makes the major difference in advertising effectiveness?

4. What should a copywriter's attitude be towards the faceless people who are being addressed?

PROJECT

List what you generally read and tell in what ways this helps contribute to your writing style. List poetry you have read and liked, novels in which you have become absorbed, plays on which you have regretted seeing the curtain come down. State in what way these have influenced your writing or your wish to write.

Chapter 4

The Language of Advertising

Because those individuals who write advertising usually confine their writing solely to advertising, they have as their only model for expression, other advertising. If they read any other form of expression it is usually for diversion — seldom for the purpose of improving their writing style. To remain current with what is happening within the field of advertising there is an unfortunate tendency among copywriters to read print advertisements — or to listen to TV and radio commercials — voraciously. As a consequence, just as they have absorbed the countless clichés of advertising by having read and heard them from childhood, their excessive reading of current advertisements, and their excessive viewing of current commercials, tend to limit their vocabulary to current advertising phrases. That in turn limits the persuasive effect of the advertising they write because it becomes recognizable as advertising and, as communication, advertising is suspect.

To avoid the language of advertising, a writer of advertising should be exposed to those forms of writing in which a conscious attempt is made by the writer to achieve freshness and originality of expression. In addition, it is useful when doing such reading to anticipate freshness of expression and when it is encountered to note it, underlining it or typing and collecting it for ready reference and, in addition, for memorizing it. Memorizing it is especially helpful and is not unlike, and tends to have the same effect as, taking an antidote to counteract the many advertising clichés absorbed over the years.

Obviously, care must be taken to avoid overly elegant or affected expression. The kind of expression to be sought must be that which gives the impression of being right, of not being a conceit, of summing up what is described in a way that is closest to being actual. This kind of expression is invariably specific, concrete, vivid. It is seldom general or abstract. It causes the reader who comes upon it to see whatever is described as never before, with illuminating clarity and an understanding that is as close as possible to actual experience. With the advent of television many copywriters assumed that to write TV commercials it was unnecessary to know anything about writing since TV commercials are spoken, not read, overlooking of course that such commercials must first be written in order to be spoken. Writing gives structure and clarity to language.

It is useful, in avoiding the language of advertising in the advertising you write, to read advertising and to listen to radio and television commercials *critically*. Look and listen for the phrases you have heard before and recognize as typical advertising phrases — such as:

Better . . .

Best . . .

Simply delicious . . .

Traditional . . .

Save time and money . . .

You'll keep asking for more . . .

Costs more but worth it . . .

Serve *your* family . . .

Goes well with any meal . . .

Add zest to any meal . . .

Priced right for your pocketbook . . .

Just what you've been waiting for . . .

Here's the best news you've seen in years . . .

All you have to do is . . .

Can you afford not to . . .

The best reason of all is . . .

Thanks to . . .

Proven effective . . .

An unbeatable combination . . .

Looks as good as it tastes . . .

Tastes as good as it looks . . .

Only (name of product) gives you . . .

The ideal gift . . .

It's virtually . . .

Makes (cooking, cleaning, ironing, etc.) more fun . . .

It's worth it . . .

You'll be proud to . . .

A lot of people think . . .

And much more . . .

Well-qualified . . .

Why not give your home (family, loved ones) . . .

Beauty that lasts . . .

Lasting beauty . . .

Minimum care . . .

You'll discover. . .

Isn't it time . . .

Taste the difference . . .

Gourmet taste (flavor, dish, dining, cuisine). . .

Here's your opportunity to . . .

Without risk . . .

Carefully chosen to . . .

Secret formula . . .

Affordable price . . .

Specially selected . . .

The hallmark of . . .

You need only . . .

Before you know it, you'll . . .

Dine like royalty . . .

You deserve the best . . .

Where else can you get . . .

Everybody knows that . . .
Has what everyone wants in a . . .
Does more than you'd expect . . .
Costs less than you think . . .
Richer . . .
Smoother . . .
Mellower . . .
Great-tasting . . .
To be treasured for years . . .
Flavor (kids, moms, dads, gourmets) love . . .
America's number one . . .
Available exclusively through . . .
For more information see your travel agent . . .
You need more than a . . .
Specialized skills . . .
There's only one way to . . .
So easy to make . . .
Follow these simple directions . . .
Healthy savings . . .
The original . . .
The one and only . . .
You'll enjoy the flavor . . .
Good — and good for you . . .
Delicious, nutritious . . .
Just like mother (or grandma) used to make . . .
Clinically proven . . .
Here's a great new . . .
That's because . . .
You'll want to . . .
If you thought that . . .
You can depend on . . .
If you like---, you'll love---
Best by test . . .
A meal in itself . . .
Unbeatable . . .

Get the (brand name) you've always wanted . . .
For people with the most discriminating tastes . . .
Here's news you've been waiting for . . .
You don't have to be rich to enjoy rich (coffee, chocolate, etc.) . . .
For a limited time only . . .
It's the smart thing to do . . .
At prices you can afford . . .
Featuring a wide selection . . .
At a price that fits your budget . . .
Our master chefs . . .
Better than ever . . .
To fit every occasion . . .
People who understand value know . . .
Now more than ever . . .
We do everything with you in mind . . .
You get special treatment . . .
It's no wonder that . . .
You'll thank your lucky stars you chose . . .
You'll find everything you need . . .
More importantly . . .
Make the switch to . . .
You'll rest easy knowing . . .
There's never been a better time to . . .
The world's most . . .
So don't put it off . . .
Confused about . . .?
You'll get more for your money . . .
Your friendly banker, baker, grocer, druggist and so on . . .
An unbeatable combination . . .
An offer you can't refuse . . .

Phrases such as these have been encountered in so many other commercial messages, that they are like old coins — what once made them valuable has been worn away through constant use. Retire them.

Retire them not only because phrases associated with advertising are suspect but because they are boring as well. If you want the advertising you write to accomplish its end purpose — to promote acceptance of what it is advocating — it must first create interest. It is for this reason that those who wish to write effective advertising copy should learn the art of storytelling. There is no product, no company, no service, no individual that cannot be made interesting. However, it is the copywriter who either makes it interesting or fails to make it interesting. To do this does not require deception or exaggeration. It simply requires writing skill and the ability to ferret out appropriate and significant information.

The writer of advertising is not unlike Cyrano de Bergerac. The writer woos for another less skilled in communication. The other must define the goal or goals but, having defined them, must surrender initiative to the communicator. The communicator, of course, must be equal to the task or give way to someone more capable. The communicator functions as an agent, and in accepting the task necessarily implies that his or her communicative ability is equal to accomplishing it. If the communicator is to merit other, similar tasks he or she must demonstrate capability and can do this in only one way — through consummate skill in the use of language.

QUESTIONS, SUBJECTS FOR DISCUSSION

1. If a copywriter is to read other advertising, in what way should it be read and why?

2. What is an effective way to keep one's writing fresh and compelling?

3. Why must even spoken commercials for radio or for television first be written?

4. What is needed to make advertising messages interesting?

5. Why should an advertising message be interesting?

6. In what way is a copywriter like Cyrano de Bergerac?

PROJECT

Read a number of newspaper and magazine advertisements; look at a number of billboards. Listen to an hour of radio commercials, an hour of TV commercials. If they are available to you or if you can obtain them, read several leaflets, booklets, or catalogues.

As you do, note down the phrases you come upon that you realize you have seen or heard in other advertisements or commercials — the cliches, the typical advertising words and phrases. Write a list of at least a dozen.

Check these, as you accumulate them, with other people to learn if they also find them typical of advertising. Ask them if they can remember similar words and similar terms. Add these to your list.

As you collect such terms, write what each attempts to say in a fresher, clearer, or more convincing manner; or re-phrase the entire sentence in which it is used to make it fresher, more interesting, and memorable.

Chapter 5

The Voice of Marketing

Marketing is a relatively recent development in the manufacture and sale of goods and services. Until almost the middle of the twentieth century it was common practice for companies to manufacture a product and then to consider ways and means of selling it. Frequently the company sought an advertising agency to study the product and come up with an advertising campaign or slogan to persuade people to buy it. This procedure resulted in a large amount of extremely unrealistic advertising — false or unfounded claims about the product, exaggerated statements about its effectiveness and, of course, numberless slogans.

Even today, more companies turn out products without first determining if a need for them exists — but the extent of that need than decide what they will manufacture by learning through research what the public wants or needs. It has been said that selling is making the customer want what the company has — in contrast to marketing which is making sure the company has what the customer wants. This statement is a great simplification of a highly complex process; however, it does state clearly and essentially the purpose of marketing.

Marketing, of course, consists not only of determining through research if a need for a product exists, and the extent of that need, so that the amount of the investment required can be justified; what features or benefits will cause most people to want it; the price those who want it will be willing to pay; the type of container that will add most to its desirability; the label design that will best identify it; and the name that will be most appropriate and easiest to pronounce and remember. Marketing includes, as well, the most effective and least expensive method of distributing the product. Only after items such as these have been considered and, if possible, tested and found worthwhile, can advertising be contemplated with any degree of assurance of promoting successfully the sale of the product. Advertising is, therefore, the *voice* of marketing—it says about the product what marketing has determined will induce the largest number of potential users of the product to try it.

In relation to what will induce people to want or to try a product, there is the strategy of "positioning." By "positioning" a product, a manufacturer does what can be done to cause it to appeal to a particular segment of the overall market. For example, it would be difficult and costly today for a manufacturer to introduce a soap to compete with Ivory soap for the total hand soap market. As a consequence, a manufacturer such as Lever Brothers produced a soap— Dove—to appeal to that segment of the facial soap market with a dry skin problem. Because of its cleansing cream content, Dove was less likely to intensify skin dryness and, as a result, could be expected to win favor of a sizable portion of this segment of the total facial "beauty bar" soap market. The product, of course, must be able to satisfy the particular need of the segment selected. When Johnson & Johnson, in the late seventies, saw the market for its baby products declining, it began running advertising calling attention to the suitability of its baby oil, baby powder, and baby shampoo for use by women. Under the circumstances there was no need to change the products in any way; the new positioning was accomplished solely through advertising.

In addition to determining what the product will be, marketing determines what its sales volume should be. Advertising is employed to help achieve this volume. It cannot be held directly responsible—too many other factors are involved: packaging, pricing, distribution, competitive activity, and so on. There is no doubt that advertising influences sales—which is why it is employed—but it is next to impossible to determine the degree of that influence. If the influence of advertising is to be measured—and, if the amount of money put behind it is to be justified, its influence *should* be measured—that measurement must be in terms of the number of logical prospects the advertising interests in trying the product, and this involves research both before and after the advertising appears.

The goal of advertising, in short, is to affect, positively or negatively, human attitudes. Insofar as these affect purchase of the product, advertising influences purchase, but in no other way.

It is for this reason that advertising, to be sound and effective, should stem from a situation analysis which acquaints the writer with exactly where the product stands in its field, what people think of it, what has previously taken place to affect that thinking; how the product compares with similar, competitive products—actually and in terms of users' opinions; its price in relation to competition, its packaging. Unless these are known to the writer, the advertising produced can positively affect its sales only through luck.

Advertising strategy differs from advertising objectives. The latter have to do with what the advertising is expected to accomplish; the former with how and in what way the objectives are to be accomplished. Shall the advertising be humorous? Shall it employ demonstrations of how the product works or accomplishes its purpose? Shall it compare the product with competitive products? Shall it quote the opinions of users? Should it be print or broadcast? The determination of the preferable advertising strategy depends largely on judgment. Strategies that were effective for similar products can be considered but, if they are, it is essential to judge their effectiveness in relation to when they were used and to what competition was doing at the time.

How good or bad the judgment is that goes into the selection of advertising strategy, the effectiveness of the strategy will depend heavily upon the quality of its execution. Advertising is essentially communication and, as the voice of marketing, the more effectively it communicates what the writer has learned it is essential to communicate, the more influential it will be in the purchase of the product. And, of course, the communication must be sufficient in volume to impress itself upon the market to which it is addressed. In this respect, a copywriter should always think in terms of a campaign, never of just a single advertisement. Thinking of several advertisements instead of just one is also conducive to a copywriter's production of concepts and phrases that may be superior to those in the original copy.

QUESTIONS, SUBJECTS FOR DISCUSSION

1. Contrast selling and marketing.

2. What elements must be considered in the development of a total marketing plan?

3. What is positioning in relation to marketing a product and what are its advantages?

4. Why is it impossible to determine the degree of influence advertising exerts in creating sales?

5. What is a situation study or analysis?

PROJECT

Select a product of any kind. Determine what its principal advantage is. Check competitive products and how they are being advertised. Then think of a way to advertise the benefit that is most likely to attract users and induce them to use it. Do not try to write an advertisement — write a copy platform, a paper on how you think the product should be advertised and why.

Chapter 6

Influence of Media

Media are not read or listened to for the advertising they carry. While they could not exist without advertising, people who read newspapers or magazines or listen to radio or watch television are not only unaware of that fact, they all too frequently consider the advertising they come upon as intrusive and therefore not welcome. The one slight exception is the informative advertising in newspapers — department store advertising, supermarket advertising, theater and restaurant advertising, classified advertising. In fact, many people buy newspapers specifically to determine what food and grocery items are available and the prices at which they can be bought. Such advertising is seldom considered annoying or an "insult to the intelligence" because it provides useful information and makes planned shopping possible. It fulfills the very purpose for which newspapers are bought — *news* coverage, particularly *local* news coverage.

Magazines, on the other hand, are bought and read primarily for the specific information they contain that is usable by or of interest to the readers who comprise their circulation. These readers vary and differ in their interests according to the editorial character and content of the magazine. In fact, magazines constitute a home library from which individuals who subscribe to them or purchase them can find and consult authorities on particular activities, interest, and hobbies. As advertisements in newspapers for department stores, supermarkets, theaters, and restaurants are looked for and welcomed, so advertisements in magazines that are *informative and helpful* are welcomed and read. It is significant in this respect that, as demonstrated by *Starch Readership Reports*, in magazines such as *Good Housekeeping, McCall's* and *Ladies' Home Journal*, as well as the "supermarket" magazines, *Woman's Day* and *Family Circle*, recipes in advertisements receive more thorough inspection from readers than the advertisements containing them.

Of all media, television offers advertisers the most effective means of presenting a product or a service — not only enabling them to show it in brilliant color and/or action but making it possible to demonstrate the product or service in use. In brief, television can bring a product or a service to "life" in the home, without the effort required to turn a page in a newspaper or a magazine or even to read. Yet repeated studies of the reaction of media audiences to advertising messages show that television commercials are considered the most irritating. The chief reason given by television viewers are (1) they interrupt the viewing of the program, (2) they are, by and large, blatant, inane, and an "insult to the intelligence," and (3) they are endlessly repetitive. At the same time, a number of commercials — a minority, it must be admitted — have been seen as interesting and informative as, and even more "entertaining" than, the program being viewed at the time of their appearance.

Of all media, radio is the most frequently used. It is listened to at all hours of the day and night for news, public comment ("talk" shows,) and, principally, for music of all varieties, from classical to rock. Ninety-nine percent of all automobiles are equipped with radios. Uncounted people carry radios with them while strolling, shopping, camping, boating, even working. More advertising messages are heard on radio than are encountered on or in any other medium. Yet few radio commercials are cited as being annoying or irritating. The reason for this may be that, unlike most other media, radio does not enlist rapt, steady, and alert attention. Radio is simply "there." It is background sound for most of its listeners. Its sound is "company," it is "companionship." Its advertising messages are part of its sound. This does not mean that they are ignored.

To sum up, advertising is least likely to be considered obtrusive or unwelcome *when it conforms to the content or the nature of the particular medium that carries it*. As stated, media are not read or listened to for the advertising they carry. As a consequence, the closer the advertising reflects the purpose for which the medium that carries it is read or listened to, the more likely it is to be welcomed and to receive the attention that the advertiser, and the copy-writer, wish it to receive.

QUESTIONS, SUBJECTS FOR DISCUSSION

1. Give the principal reason why people (1) read newspapers, (2) read magazines, (3) watch television, (4) listen to radio.

2. What singular relationship does the advertising of department stores, supermarkets, theaters, restaurants, and retail outlets generally have to the newspapers in which it appears?

3. Why is it advisable to make advertising intended for magazines informative?

4. Before television, what media were turned to primarily for entertainment? Cite examples of their content or programming.

5. Why do people spend as much time as they do viewing television? In view of this, what should be the general nature of television commercials?

PROJECT

In a local newspaper, a women's service magazine, an hour of prime time television, and a half hour of radio, check the advertising messages for their harmony with the reason why readers, viewers, or listeners (in your opinion) turned to each of the media. List these as well as those not in harmony with the editorial or program content as well as your reaction to each, being careful to define what you consider the nature and objective of the editorial and the program content.

Chapter 7

Print Advertising

There is as much difference between print advertising and broadcast advertising as there is between the novel and the play. It is, however, considerably simpler for the aspiring copywriter to acquire proficiency in both print advertising and broadcast advertising than it is for the literary tyro to master both novel-writing and playwriting—if only because the advertisement as a form of communication is itself considerably simpler than either the novel or the play. Many would refer to advertising as trivial by comparison, and it might be so considered in terms of its overall contribution. However, advertising has become so dominant a factor in communications that there is some justification for comparing it with more serious forms of writing. It is also likely that, if it *were* looked upon as one of the more dominant arms of communications, its writing might be more respected and, as a result, more respectful of human sensitivity than it is. This might also improve its efficacy when used to further social as well as commercial aims.

Reading a print advertisement of any kind—a magazine advertisement, a newspaper advertisement, a direct mail letter, a booklet, a leaflet—requires more mental effort than hearing a radio commercial or viewing a television spot. There is a need, therefore, on the part of the copywriter to make the potential reader not simply willing but eager to expend the effort and the time required to absorb what the message has to say—not just partially but in its entirety. In fact, the copywriter must be sensitively aware of this need and the problem it imposes in order to spend sufficient effort and time to bring into being an initial statement—or headline—that will arouse attention and interest to the degree that the reader will be impelled to read the copy that follows.

To accomplish this, the initial statement — or headline — must do more than simply stir the reader's curiosity. It must cause the reader to determine to spend the time required and the effort to read the message *because he or she is convinced it will be advantageous to do so, and will be of personal value.* To be able to achieve this demands judgment on the part of the copywriter about what will be of prime interest to the reader and how to maintain that interest to the end of the message. This arousal of interest must be sufficiently intense to overcome other activities open to the reader as well as other advertisements competing for attention.

The creator of print advertising has still other problems in transmitting a message. These have to do with design and typography. The act of reading must be made as easy as possible or the reader's attention will be lost regardless of what the message has to say. Too small a type size, for example, can create eye-strain and discourage further reading. It has been established through many years of research that sheer mechanical devices — such as long lines of type, lengthy paragraphs, "reverse" type, among many others — cause many readers not only to stop reading but not even to start.

If an advertisement is to affect a reader's attitude, it must first be noticed and then read thoroughly. To bring this about, a copywriter must not only create a headline that attracts readers and write copy that arouses and holds their interest, the copywriter — as well as the art director — should know how to design an advertisement in a way that is most likely to have it noticed and set in type in such a way as to encourage reading of the copy.

Fortunately, studies of the reading of both newspaper advertising and magazine advertising have been conducted since the early thirties. The purpose of these studies was to determine the percentage of circulation that (a) "noted" the message and (b) read its copy. These studies were called "readership reports" and were bought by advertisers and advertising agencies to learn how well their advertisement was noted and read in comparison with how well competitors' advertisements were noted and read. Few advertisers and advertising agencies were aware that by observing the design and the typography of advertisements that were given high noting and reading percentages, it was possible to discover the *kind* of design and typography that would help *assure* high noting and reading.

Because of the importance of design and typography to the noting and reading of print advertising, the chapters that immediately follow this one list the most effective ways of designing print advertising and setting it in type to achieve high noting and reading.

QUESTIONS, SUBJECTS FOR DISCUSSION

1. What is the major difference between print advertising and broadcast advertising?

2. What particular responsibility does this difference impose on the writer of print advertising?

3. What relationship does the headline of a print advertisement have to this responsibility?

4. In order to meet this responsibility, how should the copywriter conceive the headline in relation to potential readers?

5. In gaining the attention of potential readers, what competition does the copywriter face?

PROJECT

Find and read five advertisements in a magazine and five advertisements in a newspaper. After reading each, ask yourself which interests you most in the product advertised and which interests you least and try to explain why. After doing this have ten individuals who might buy the product read the ads and ask each which of the advertisements provoked the most interest and why.

Chapter 8

The Design of Print Advertising

Any print advertising consists of four essential elements — copy, illustration, layout (or design), and type. What strikes the eye first in print advertising is the overall appearance of the advertisement. As a consequence, the first element of print advertising that either attracts the potential reader or fails to is the element of design.

Ultimately, design is the province of the layout planner or art director. However, the writer contributes to the design in no small measure not only by what is written but by how it is written. Whatever the headline says strongly affects the illustration that will accompany it. If the copywriter does the copy as a cartoon sequence, the layout director is almost inevitably compelled to design the advertisement as a cartoon. If the advertisement is done as a cartoon sequence, the copy generally will be lettered rather than set in type and will appear in balloons issuing from the mouths of the cartoon characters rather than in orderly columns of type. However the design comes about, more than a half-century of research into the influence of design in print advertising exists for its creators to call on.

The research was initiated by a number of individuals in the early 1930s, including George Gallup and Daniel Starch. It is the latter by whose name so-called readership research is usually identified and the design principles derived from the research are usually referred to as Starch techniques.

Both Starch and Gallup undertook their research because, then as now, advertisers were charged for both magazine and newspaper space in relation to the circulation of the particular magazine or newspaper. Obviously the greater the circulation, the higher the cost per black and white page or per agate line—the basic cost formulae for magazines and for newspapers.

It occurred to both Starch and Gallup that charging for space in terms of circulation of the medium was extremely arbitrary because while publishers, through the Audit Bureau of Circulations, could guarantee the number of individuals who bought the media they published, they could in no way guarantee that every advertisement in every issue would be seen and read by the total circulation. What Starch and Gallup chose to determine was not only how many purchasers of the media saw the advertisements but the extent to which those who saw them read them.

Starch and Gallup also reasoned that the more people who saw and read an advertisement—particularly the more who read it thoroughly—the more likely the advertisement was to generate sales and so the greater value per dollar spent for the space the advertiser bought could be achieved. As a consequence, to promote the purchase of his service by advertisers, Starch initially claimed that he was measuring advertising *effectiveness*. Challenged by the author on the basis that if he were measuring actual advertising effectiveness he should be able to predict sales results, Starch modified his claim to that of being able to determine for advertisers how many readers their advertising attracted and the extent to which those readers read the message.

To arrive at the number of readers he should interview to obtain greatest accuracy, Starch chose samples from 100 to 10,000 and found he obtained a factor of stability at 200. Since 1932, the organization he founded—now known as Starch-INRA-Hooper—has interviewed many millions of readers, and Starch findings in that time have neither varied nor changed. The advertising designs that obtained top noting and top reading in the early 1930s still obtain top noting and top reading today and those that obtained least noting and least reading obtain least noting and least reading today.

While most of the advertisers who have subscribed to *Starch Readership Reports* have done so to determine how well their advertisements have performed in attracting and holding readers in relation to their competitors' advertisements, a number of individuals analyzed Starch findings to learn exactly what elements of design could be employed in the preparation of a piece of advertising to ensure major attention and reading. While Starch-INRA-Hooper has covered a number of such design principles in some of its promotions, and while a number of individual research people have called attention to some of these principles in articles they have written and had published in the trade press, no readily available source of all of them exists, and a review of print advertising will show that in excess of 99 percent of all advertising reveals little if any awareness of them.

Some advertisers and some advertising people minimize the value of high readership scores — on the basis that most direct response or coupon-carrying advertisements, including those known to produce highest coupon returns, when studied by Starch, are shown to attract very few readers. There is a reason for this, however, which will be covered in the chapter on direct response advertising. Since advertising is to be seen and read, the use of Starch findings in the design of print advertising is definitely useful.

QUESTIONS, SUBJECTS FOR DISCUSSION

1. What are the four elements of an advertisement?

2. Which of these is necessarily seen first?

3. Who is responsible for the overall design of an advertisement?

4. Does the copywriter in any way influence the design of an advertisement? If so, how? Give an example.

5. What is "readership research"?

6. Name two individuals who initiated readership research.

7. When did they initiate it?

8. What is the Audit Bureau of Circulation?

9. If two advertisers pay the same price for a full page black-and-white advertisement in a magazine, do both obtain the same value from their advertising? If not, why not?

10. Why is the readership research advisable?

PROJECT

Interview, personally or by telephone, three individuals in one or more of the occupations listed below and ask each if that individual can tell you how to improve the attention and reading of a print advertisement in a magazine:

- Art director in an advertising agency
- Copywriter in an advertising agency
- Advertising manager of a company

Write a paper giving the findings of your interviews commenting on what you have been told about the creation and design of an advertisement and whether or not what you were told is based on research or simply the opinion of the individual.

Chapter 9

Starch Techniques

Starch Readership Reports, if studied, reveal certain principles of design that cause more individuals to notice magazine and newspaper advertisements, outdoor posters, catalogues, brochures, and other forms of print advertising than is possible to achieve through sheer personal predilection.

To the extent that they disclose particular patterns for increasing the noting and reading of advertising, they can be said to be restrictive. But they are no more restrictive than a rectangular canvas is to an artist or a block of marble of a given size is to a sculptor. As a matter of fact, they provide clues to particular patterns of design and typography that cause more readers to notice an advertisement and read more of its message.

The influence of these patterns in attracting attention and holding interest has not changed since Daniel Starch first introduced his *Readership Reports* in 1934. If it had, their validity might be questioned. But the patterns and principles that obtained higher noting and greater reading of advertising in 1934 can be predicted confidently to assure higher noting and greater reading today. And do.

Although the Starch organization (Starch-INRA-Hooper) has covered some of the design methods for improving noting and reading in its promotion material, it has never covered all. David Ogilvy in *Ogilvy on Advertising* has covered a number, but still not all. In listing most of them, the caution must be made that these simply increase the noting and reading of various forms of print advertising, primarily magazine advertisements. Their use does not in any way make poorly written copy even a trifle more effective. They **do, however, expose well-written** advertisements to a larger audience than it might otherwise obtain, and increase the amount of the copy that is read.

Here, then, is a list of Starch techniques for improving the noting and reading of print advertising.

LAYOUT DESIGN

Orderly, geometric design obtains greater noting than cluttered elements.

Liberal use of white space attracts and holds more readers than crowding the elements.

An illustration that is rectangular and occupies five-eighths of the upper part of the advertisement increases noting.

An object in outline and surrounded by white space occupying five-eighths of the upper part of an advertisement will obtain high noting.

Photographs obtain higher noting than either drawings or paintings — except in the illustrations of women's fashions. Copy set under photographs obtains very high reading if it does not exceed four lines. This is the *Life* magazine or picture-caption technique. If used, all photos should be the same size and should be directly across from and under one another.

Advertisements done as cartoons usually obtain higher noting and reading than any other type of technique or design. All copy must be contained within balloons issuing from the mouths of the individuals portrayed.

Illustrations featuring women, babies, flowers, or other items liked, worn, or used by women attract more female readers than male readers. Conversely, illustrations featuring men, automobiles, guns, and items generally liked, used, or worn by men attract more male readers than female readers. This is important to bear in mind when the target audience is either men or women.

HEADLINES

The best position for noting and reading headlines is under the main illustration. The next best position is over the illustration. When there is no illustration, the headline should be set in large type above the copy in plenty of white space. Also headlines set totally in capital letters get less reading than headlines set in caps and lower case.

Headlines set in italics obtain less reading than headlines set in roman type.

Headlines set in one line — or, at the most, two — obtain more thorough reading than headlines set in three lines or more.

Headlines obtain less noting and reading when they are printed in so-called reverse type — white against a black or any other color background except yellow. Headlines printed in black on white obtain the highest noting and reading.

Headlines printed over part of an illustration obtain less noting than headlines with nothing behind them. This applies as well to headlines crowded by other elements of the advertisement. The more white space around a headline, the better the headline will be noted and read.

TYPOGRAPHY

Text set in narrow columns — no longer than an alphabet and a half (or 39 letter spaces) — obtains more thorough reading than text set in wider measure or full width of page.

Text set in short paragraphs gets better reading than text set in lengthy paragraphs.

A short first paragraph is more likely to start the reading of the copy than a long first paragraph.

Text set in serif type is read more thoroughly than text set in sans serif type.

Text printed in reverse — or in white letters against a dark background — will usually obtain from 10 to 30 percent less reading than text printed in black on white.

Yellow is the only color against which text can be printed that will not reduce the amount of reading it gets.

Long copy is more likely to be read when interspersed with sub-heads either in roman or italic letters set throughout its length and usually in boldface.

Setting an occasional word in text in italics or underlining tends to increase reading of the copy in general. However, setting the text totally in italics—or underlining it in toto—will definitely reduce the amount of attention given it.

If particular paragraphs are to be emphasized, numbering them will result in their obtaining more reading than preceding them with large black dots or paragraph marks.

Using white space between paragraphs rather than having the text set solidly will obtain higher reading for the message.

"Widows"—or final lines of paragraphs that do not occupy full width of the column—tend to invite more reading of the copy than text in which every line, including the last line of every paragraph, is full width of the column.

These findings apply not just to magazine advertising but to all forms of print advertising.

When the *Life Magazine* or picture-caption pattern is used, all pictures should be rectangular and of equal size, all captions should appear in no more than four lines and the first two or three words should be in boldface type.

Q.E.D.

Whether an advertisement is intended to be read by consumers or by specialists, certain principles apply in the writing and design of the advertisement that can be ignored only to the detriment of the advertisement's performance in obtaining top noting and reading.

The following two industrial advertisements, which ran in the same trade magazines and addressed the same management audience, dramatically illustrate, by the Starch scores they obtained, how sound it is to write and design advertising messages according to the findings of *Starch Readership Reports* as well as of direct response advertising.

Each message was addressed to users of metal and metal products and offered services enabling these users to reduce inventory costs by providing production-ready items made of a specific metal — either steel or aluminum. This chapter has informed you of the role of illustration and headline in obtaining reader attention and interest in reading the copy message. Notice how vague and general the illustration and headline of the Consolidated Aluminum ad are and how direct and specific those of the Steel Service Center Institute are — and notice the startling difference in Starch scores. Each advertiser paid the same amount of money for the page, which was based on the circulation of the magazine. However, look at the percentage of that circulation attracted by one ad and the percentage attracted by the other. It *pays* to know what you are doing.

WHO KNOWS WHAT EVIL LURKS IN YOUR INVENTORY SHEET?

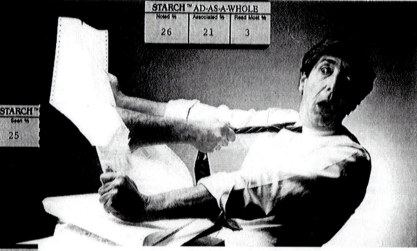

You can't spend sheet and plate. Or pay your bills with stacks of aluminum. But when you've got a rush order, you can't afford to wait weeks for delivery, either.

Next time this old dilemma rears its ugly head, reach for the phone and call a Consolidated Aluminum affiliated service center.

Whether you need an old standby or a high-performance alloy, service centers can help you trim production lead times without tying up assets months in advance. Or paying through the nose for storage space.

And since they handle custom shearing, slitting, blanking and punching, they can help eliminate waste and scrap—while reducing your personnel and equipment costs significantly. too.

As one of the nation's major aluminum producers, Consolidated offers a wide variety of products, 12 plants,

and an outstanding delivery record. Plus a history of dedication to the service center industry.

If that's the kind of backup you're looking for, why not call our Sales Service Manager, Tom Ellis, at (800) 848-5200 today.

He'll put you in touch with someone who can exorcise your inventory evil once and for all. Someone who'll keep your cash flow flowing and your cost of possession in check. The aluminum service center in your area affiliated with Consolidated.

CONSOLIDATED ALUMINUM

Service Center Division
P.O. Box 164
Hannibal, Ohio 43931

The difference between these could save you about $50,000.

They look the same. And, in most respects, they are the same.

But these two flame-cut steel pieces don't cost the same.

You see, a part made in-house by the manufacturer has costs that go far beyond the piece itself. Including material inventory, overhead, labor, and pre-production processing.

These are the hidden Costs of Possession that can add as much as $50,000 to every $100,000 of steel inventory you own.

And yet the same piece, supplied by a member company of the Steel Service Center Institute, could reduce your Costs of Possession dramatically. You avoid the labor, storage, and processing costs of a large metal inventory. Not to mention taxes, insurance, scrap loss, and the high cost of interest.

What's more, Steel Service Center Institute members can handle initial pre-production processing, such as slitting or flame-cutting, efficiently and economically.

They can also complement Materials Requirements Planning (MRP) systems by offering precise quantities to match your production schedule.

If you are flame-cutting pieces like this yourself or doing other pre-production processing, call your local Steel Service Center member for help with a Cost of Possession evaluation.

It could make quite a difference.

Your nearby Steel Service Center Institute member can help reduce your inventory costs and supply you with the metal you need, production-ready.

Steel Service Center Institute

Steel Service Center Institute, 1600 Terminal Tower, Cleveland, Ohio 44113
For Information, Circle 117

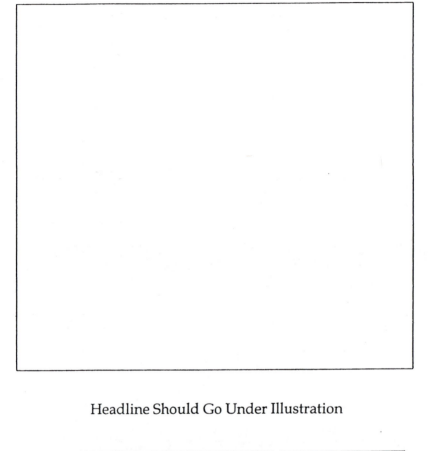

Headline Should Go Under Illustration

Signature Goes Here

Go to an island where you'll be understood, know

you'll enjoy the food – and still be on an island!

Go to Bermuda!

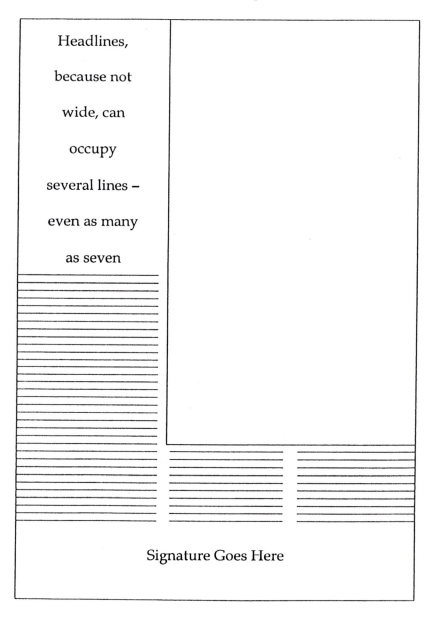

Headlines,

because not

wide, can

occupy

several lines –

even as many

as seven

Signature Goes Here

Headline becomes

the illustration

Signature

QUESTIONS, SUBJECTS FOR DISCUSSION

1. What is the best position in an advertisement for the main illustration? How much of the page should it occupy?

2. What are the two best positions for the headline?

3. What is the optimum width for a column of type?

4. What is the best way to call attention to particular paragraphs in an advertisement?

5. Why do you suppose photographs obtain better noting than paintings or drawings?

6. What can be done to increase the reading of long copy?

7. In a picture-caption advertisement, what is the maximum length to which the copy should be held for greatest reading?

PROJECT

Find an advertisement in a magazine which, according to what you have just read, violates Starch principles. Re-design it according to Starch findings and explain why you have re-designed it as you have.

Chapter 10

Creating Print Advertising

There are two phases in creating print advertising — as there are in the creation of all advertising. The first is the planning stage, the second the stage of writing and designing. The first consists of determining *what* is to be said; the second, *how* it should be said. Both, in their way, are equally important.

What is said relates to whether or not the item advertised will be found of sufficient worth or value or benefit to be considered for purchase. *How* what is said is phrased and presented will stimulate or fail to stimulate a general emotional reaction in the reader. The latter is the same element that makes one salesman more welcome, more interesting, more compelling than another. It is an element that perhaps can best be described as style or personality. It is a personal element that causes the message to be interesting and to inspire not just confidence but belief in what it says, and an urge to do what it suggests. It is, as the song has it, "almost like falling in love."

Because what is said is basic and fundamental and comes before how it is said, let us consider first the elements of the planning stage. In some way the copywriter must learn as much as possible about the product — why it was made, how it is made, what has happened to it since its introduction; what improvements have been added to it; why they were added to it; what share of market it has achieved; how this occurred, rapidly or slowly; what has happened to share recently; how it compares to competitors' share; if it is less, why is it less; and if it is more, why is it more. The copywriter must learn, in short, the entire history of the product or service as well as of its competition.

The copywriter must learn, in addition, what users think of the

51

product, the reaction of non-users, what research, if any, has re-
vealed about consumer attitudes towards it, the kinds of people that
tend to prefer it, their educational level, their income level, their
geographical area — urban, suburban, rural; their activities, their
hobbies; anything about them that makes them particularly suitable
to be considered its target market.

To sum up, the planning stage results in learning as much as
possible about the product and of the people who are most likely to
find it of use to them. Out of these two sources of information
comes the advertising *objective* — what to say about the product that
is most likely to interest the target market and induce it to purchase
the product.

To a marked degree the determination of the target audience will
suggest what medium or media might prove most efficient in carrying the message at lowest cost per thousand individuals reached.
How what is said is said, however, can also suggest the medium or
media to carry the message most effectively. If the copy strategy is
to rely heavily on demonstration, television might be indicated. If
description at length is necessary, then a print medium would be
preferable. Not infrequently the kind of advertising decided upon
dictates the nature of the medium employed which emphasizes the
importance of how the message is told.

Research, study of the product and its largest audience, are essential to determination of the advertising objective. The strategy
employed in doing this, however, is considerably more subjective
and involves creative perception, experience, and judgment, even
when research is ultimately employed to determine — as best it can
be determined — the assumed effectiveness of the strategy.

Such research might entail exposure of the advertising to a representative sample of the target audience or actual publication of the
advertising in a test market or in test markets. However, while research may be effective post facto, no amount of research can be
counted upon to achieve the unparalleled communication of which
creative perception alone is productive.

It should not be assumed that creative perception of high order
cannot be developed. The capacity to produce exceptional advertising — like the capacity to write poetry — is not an accident of birth. It
comes, first of all, from becoming acquainted with communication.

It grows as knowledge of great art grows and interest in exploring it totally grows. Constant application of what is learned eventually results in skill and facility. This differs in no way from developing skill and facility in sculpture, painting, or musical performance. The personal element of style comes about by analyzing and, for a time, copying the work of those who have excelled. It is for this reason that beginning copywriters should expose themselves to most advertising only for the purpose of observing and being able to identify its faults, for most of it is not only faulty but betrays a lack of skill and even competence. The exceptional creator of advertising becomes exceptional by never being fully satisfied with what is created, by being fanatically determined to produce exceptional work and by improving, improving, improving until there is no time remaining for further improvement. Few of us have the courage or determination to bring ourselves to this stage. When we do, however, the inner and outer rewards are as exceptional as the achievement itself.

How do most advertisements begin and what is required to bring them into being? Pencil and paper appear to be the preferable tools. These can be used for scribbling layout designs ("thumb-nails"), headlines, or actual copy. Different individuals employ different ways of getting out of their minds what first evolves there. A writer may prefer to work alone with the muse or to exchange views with an art director. Seldom if ever do exceptional creative ideas issue from a committee. The ideas that evolve from committee collaboration almost invariably reflect the imaginative level of the least capable members of the committee and seldom rise above that.

Once a headline and a suitable layout design are achieved and found promising, rough copy is written and a rough layout pencilled. Both may be re-done and revised several, even many, times. It is seldom advisable to consider what is first done as a work of genius. It may be. It is fruitful, however, to "polish" the first effort, to study it for possible improvement. It is useful to try other approaches—if only for comparison. The creative process is demanding, even exhausting, but its finest achievement comes from never being satisfied—even with obviously superior work, one should never cease to think of ways in which clearer, more exciting, more compelling communication might be brought into being. There is no other way to outstanding advertising.

QUESTIONS, SUBJECTS FOR DISCUSSION

1. What are the two phases in creating advertising of any kind?
2. What is the reason for the first phase?
3. What should be learned about the product?
4. What should be learned about competition?
5. How is the target market determined?
6. What does the second phase in creating advertising add to the first phase?
7. To what is the second phase comparable in a human being?
8. How are advertisements generally brought into physical being?

PROJECT

Obtain books in which advertisements considered to have been "outstanding" have been published—such as Julian Watkins' *The Hundred Best Advertisements*. Analyze several of them and write a paper explaining why you think they were considered outstanding and if you believe they would be considered so today.

How to Analyze an Advertisement

1. As you read it, underline those words that mention an advantage of the product, a benefit it offers, and evidence that it is effective.
2. Determine if it has any advantages you believe are more likely to interest readers than what you have underlined.
3. Does the headline clearly call attention to and acquaint the reader with either the advantages of the product, its benefits, or both?

4. Is the layout clean, uncluttered, and designed according to Starch principles of readership?

5. Has the copy any cliches that make it read and appear as if it were "just another advertisement?"

6. Does the advertisement look sufficiently different from advertisements for competitive products?

7. Can you conceive of a more effective way to write the copy and do the layout? If so, do it.

Chapter 11

Magazine Advertising

The average magazine rack, wherever magazines are sold, reveals very clearly and comprehensively the nature of the medium. Leafing through the various periodicals displayed can prove highly instructive to the copywriter with an assignment to write advertising copy for publication in a magazine. Each of the magazines is thoroughly devoted to providing information concerning one particular subject. As a result, the magazine is bought by individuals involved with that subject.

Because of that, magazines are the most selective of the major media. Through them an advertiser is able to reach individuals most likely to comprise the so-called "target" market for a certain product. The magazine offers the advertiser an additional advantage — not only does it effectively cull from the millions of consumers in the country those with a particular interest, its editorial content tends to transfer that interest to the advertising. To benefit the reader, the advertising must be as informative as the editorial content surrounding it. Because of this, advertising can be made factual and as full of detail about the product as may be necessary to create sufficient interest for the reader to purchase it.

While magazines are usually devoted to one subject, they cover it in a variety of ways with, for example, regular features written by staff members as well as special articles written by professional writers, authorities, or celebrities. Advertisers can benefit from similar treatment of their advertising since it is what obviously induces readers to read. While advertisers occasionally employ celebrities in "testimonial" advertisements, their use of a celebrity seldom goes beyond a statement testifying to the celebrity's use of the product.

It is unfortunate, particularly in magazines, that advertisements are invariably written *as* advertisements with, as a consequence, less interest for the readers than the editorial material. If the advertisements that appear in a magazine had to meet the approval of the editor, it is unlikely that very many would be found acceptable. A good discipline for the copywriter to employ, when writing an advertisement for appearance in a magazine, is not only to read the editorial content of the magazine first but to write the copy as if it had to meet the approval of the editor. In this respect, copywriters can learn a great deal and improve their writing style by writing articles for publication. The discipline required can also make them more conscious of the incredible number of clichés that advertising copywriters tend to employ — largely because they read more advertising than any other form of writing. Attempting to write for publications can, in addition, sharpen the mental focus of writers of advertising. As copywriters they tend to see their major purpose as that of persuading as many readers as possible to buy the product about which they are writing. They are aware that advertising is a highly competitive field and if the agency for which they are working does not provide its clients with effective "selling" copy, the clients may assign their accounts to other agencies. Regardless of the motivating factor, thinking primarily in terms of *selling* the product rather than in terms of interesting people in it inclines copywriters to concentrate on claims demonstrating superiority over other products, even to exaggerating these to bring about purchase. Emphasizing product superiority to the exclusion of benefits to the reader becomes less effective with each passing year as the public is over-exposed to such claims and dismisses them as "just advertising."

A writer who is primarily concerned with writing clear and accurate communication is far more likely to build a continuing market for the product than the writer who is primarily concerned with so-called "selling." This is far more likely to happen because the writing will inescapably create a more favorable "image" for the product and actually prove more persuasive. The focus of the writing is sharper and, because it is, the conception of the product created by the advertisement is more likely to establish an appreciation of it *for what it actually is*, and only in this way can a buyer of the product become a genuinely satisfied and loyal customer.

It is difficult for a manufacturer to comprehend how dedication to vivid and accurate communication can contribute more to business — and sales — in the long run than the sheer making of powerful claims. It can, however, and does, because of that moment of truth when a reader of advertising *tries* the product. If it meets the expectations the advertising has stimulated in the reader, the attitude he or she has toward the product and the company will be considerably more favorable than if it fails to.

And this applies, of course, not just to magazine advertising but to all forms of advertising. It is simply more possible in magazine advertising because magazines are a medium in which competent writing can better be exercised than in almost any other medium.

PATTERN TO BE USED IN TYPING COPY

Advertiser
Medium
Size of ad
B & W or 4 C

HEADLINE IS CENTERED AND IN CAPS

<u>If there is a subhead, place it under the
headline and underline it simply to
distinguish it from copy</u>

If the headline offers a benefit, the benefit should be restated in the first paragraph. Keep paragraphs short.

Develop the story of the benefit and, of course, provide evidence giving readers assurance if they use the product they will benefit from doing so.

Each sentence should be sufficiently informative to induce the reader to want to read the next sentence to learn more. Always be factual and employ specific words, not generalities.

Subheads in bold italics
can boost interest

While many people say they do not like and will not read long copy, this occurs only if the copy does not excite and hold their interest — not so much through its literary quality as through what it says that is of interest to them.

Before closing, the copy should make clear that the product is superior to competition and in exactly what way it is superior.

If the product has a price advantage or costs less than competitive products, mention this. If it is more expensive say so and justify its higher cost.

If the product is available only in certain kinds of outlets, mention that fact. If it is generally available, there is no need to say so. Avoid clichés such as "at your favorite supermarket."

PRODUCT OR COMPANY NAME AT BOTTOM

QUESTIONS, SUBJECTS FOR DISCUSSION

1. What is the basic function of a magazine which distinguishes it from all other media?

2. What does this make possible in terms of the kind of people an advertiser wants to reach?

3. As a consequence, what kind of advertising is likely to prove most effective in magazines?

4. What is the "image" or "personality" of a product, and how is it brought into being?

5. What can a copywriter gain by attempting to write articles for magazines?

6. In what way or ways is a copywriter's dedication to the development of writing skill more important to an advertiser than sheer dedication to "selling" the advertiser's product through

possibly exaggerated claims about the product's value or efficacy?

7. Do you think it is possible to convince an advertiser of this? If so, how would you do it?

PROJECT

Select any magazine. Scan its editorial as well as its advertising content. Relate the relative value, in your opinion, of each to the readers of the magazine. Select those advertisements you believe readers will find of most interest in terms of the useful information they provide. Determine the percentage of these advertisements in relation to the total number of advertisements in the issue. Explain why you find the advertisements you selected preferable to the other advertisements in the issue.

Chapter 12

Consumer Products Advertising

The type of advertising that generally comes to mind when the word "advertising" is mentioned is consumer products advertising — promoting products and services used by most individuals in their daily lives, such as food products, non-prescription drugs, clothing, grooming aids, refrigerators, clothes washers, and dishwashers.

All these are promoted by brand names and the advertising promoting each is used to create a preference in consumers, in every category of product and service, for one particular brand. It has been assumed by manufacturers and processors of products and by distributors of services that brand preference results primarily from instilling belief in an advantage or a benefit superior to what competitive products or services have to offer. This has led to the school of the "unique selling proposition" in which a singular quality of the product or service, not to be found in other products or services, is featured. The quality featured, of course, must be not only unique but desirable.

Finding a unique and desirable quality becomes a difficult task in so-called "parity" products — such as cigarettes, coffees, analgesics, and many processed foods. As a result, all too frequently uniqueness is found by describing a common quality with a coined and scientific-sounding name. The preferable course is to learn — through research — what in the product is preferred by most people and is most likely to induce them to buy it, and to present what you have learned in an interesting and believable way.

To invest the appeal employed with added cogency, early advertising texts suggested that it be addressed to one or more of the "basic human emotions" — sex, acquisitiveness, fear, and so on.

Many advertisements of the time did just that, with the unfortunate result that they appeared contrived and brought about the reaction to advertising that exists today: that it is essentially exploitative and therefore cannot be accepted as being "the truth, the whole truth, and nothing but the truth."

No small number of modern texts suggest a thorough background in the behavioral sciences. However, delving too deeply into the demographics and psychographics of the market tends to cause a writer to think in terms of manipulating readers rather than communicating with them as with a friend or an acquaintance. If the writer is satisfied with the worth of the product—and in what aspects of the product that worth lies—the primary problem is writing in such a way that the product can, in a sense, be "sampled" and understood by the reader. In actual sales, few activities have been found to interest an individual in a product or a service like sampling or demonstration. These involve the reader. They make it clear, as words seldom can, what the product, if purchased, will mean to or do for that reader. Advertising that can vicariously convey sampling or demonstration can arouse a reader's interest much more compellingly than mere verbal claims. The opinion of a respected authority or the findings of an actual and named test (not an unidentified one) comes close to accomplishing the same end—provided that the writer writes of the authority or of the test and the conclusions of each as if doing an article on the subject instead of an advertisement. There is no reason a copywriter cannot write advertising in a way to avoid its *sounding* like advertising. A good copywriter needs training and experience, of course, in other forms of writing. But what is needed more than anything else is a respect for the reader as another human being with an insatiable interest in helpful information and a resentment of misrepresentation and misleading information.

In person-to-person selling, few activities have been found more likely to provide conviction in the product's worth than sampling (as with a food product) or demonstration (as with a mechanical product.) To sample or demonstrate a product in print advertising and the written word requires proof that somebody has sampled or tried the product and actually experienced the benefits or advantages claimed. Simply showing a pleased expression on a nameless model's face will not convey conviction. An actual consumer must be used and identified, not merely by initials, but by name, address (town or city) and even by telephone number. Of course, a respected authority can also be employed.

The manner in which the message is written can also contribute to its believability. If, like an article, it states why the sampling was conducted and the lack of bias of the company conducting it, it is more likely to be believed than if the results only are given. In no other medium is this more possible than in magazines—which are bought for the information they contain, allow presentation at length, and contribute their own degree of respect as sources of reliable information. Advertising that does the same inevitably enjoys a similar reader reaction.

QUESTIONS, SUBJECTS FOR DISCUSSION

1. What is a unique selling proposition?

2. Can the mere uniqueness of a selling proposition cause an increase in sales or preference of the product advertised? If not, why not?

3. What is a pre-occupation on the part of the writer with demographics and psychographics likely to do to the copy he or she writes?

4. What should be the extent of knowledge of a product by someone who is going to write advertising for it?

5. What successful methods of interesting potential customers can be applied to advertising to make it more compelling?

PROJECT

In a consumer magazine, select an advertisement that because of the manner of its writing could be dismissed as being "just advertising." Re-write and re-design it in a way you believe readers will find it helpful, useful, and conducive to their wanting the product.

Chapter 13

Headlines

As has been stated already, advertisements in newspapers and magazines are initially observed as an *entity* as the page on which they appear is turned to. According to Starch, color advertisements attract 50 percent more readers than advertisements in black and white. (The reference is to full page ads.) The Starch findings also demonstrate that the more people who are attracted to an advertisement, the more likely they are to read its copy. The design of print advertisements is, therefore, important, including the use or non-use of color.

However, of more importance than the sheer number of people who are attracted to an advertisement is the number of *potential purchasers* attracted to it, the so-called target market. The determining factor affecting how many potential purchasers are attracted to an ad and induced to read it is the headline. While the product which the readers may purchase may be mentioned in the copy or even illustrated, it is the headline — because of the size of the type in which it is set or its placement on the page — in which readers can most immediately learn of the advantages or benefits available. Also, as Starch findings indicate, an average of *six times as many readers read headlines as read copy*. It is chiefly because of these reasons that headlines should be written:

1. To attract readers most likely to be interested in the product.
2. To be clear and specific so that there is no misunderstanding the benefits available.
3. To **establish,** if possible, the uniqueness and preferability of the product to competitive products.

There is a strong temptation, indeed an urge, among both beginning and even seasoned copywriters to write headlines that are "clever" or that excite curiosity. But "clever" as well as curiosity-arousing headlines do not necessarily stimulate interest in the product and the major purpose of an advertisement is to create interest. A "clever" headline occasionally (but only occasionally) states an advantage or a benefit more incisively than that advantage might be expressed in everyday language. A headline for the original Volkswagen "bug" is a good example: *Eases gas pains.* This was bound to attract people for whom the Volkswagen was intended – those who wanted economical transportation. In addition, because of its uniqueness and memorability, such a headline is likely not only to make a deeper impression but to have the benefit it promises more intimately associated with the product than if it were stated prosaically. However, if a choice must be made between stating a claim clearly and having it "clever" but vague, choose clarity.

Similarly, a curiosity-provoking headline can select potential users if the curiosity it arouses is curiosity to learn what the product or service has to offer. Such a headline might make the statement: *Six reasons why a Volkswagen lets you drive farther between gas stations.* Notice, however, that a benefit *is* clearly stated. This would also be true of one of the most provocative kind of headlines: those beginning with How to: *How to stop at gas stations less frequently.*

A short headline is more likely to be read than a long headline. But remember, the number of people who see and read a headline is of less importance than the number of logical prospects attracted by it. The content of the headline, in short, should do what the content of a magazine does – attract readers of a particular kind. A headline comes to a writer, generally, as part of the overall strategy adopted. Whether a headline is "directive" or "curiosity-provoking" matters little if its main purposes are accomplished – of attracting the attention of major prospects by stating a benefit of the product or service, so that the reader wants to read the copy for more information; or, if not, leaving the reader with a clear and favorable conception of the product.

Whatever the type of headline, the words used in it should be specific and concrete rather than general and abstract – which, of course, applies as well to the words used in the copy or text. Use rose, daffodil, or violet in preference to flower; white bread, bacon, baked beans to food; claw hammer, cold chisel, linesman's pliers to tool. General and abstract words convey less meaning and certainly are less clear than specific and concrete words.

Quite relative to this is general semantics, a lingual system propounded by Alfred Korzybski in his book *Science and Sanity: An Introduction to Non-Artistotelian Systems and General Semantics*, published in 1933. Korzybski saw language as a map of reality and stated that if the map were incorrect or not clearly understood, reality could not be comprehended. His concept of the "structural differential" in description should be borne in mind by copywriters. In effect, cows can be most positively described by being called just that — cows. If they are referred to as cattle, then bulls, heifers, or steers might be inferred as well as cows. If the word livestock is employed, chickens, pigs, lambs, and horses may be inferred. Korzybski's caution to users of language was to be as specific as possible in communicating if auditors or readers are to understand exactly what is being communicated.

As for what the headline says, it should state, specifically, the principal advantage or benefit of whatever is being advertised — if possible a unique benefit or advantage, something that sets it apart from competition and makes it seem more desirable than the competition. There are few products that do not have some advantage and provide some benefit. Even when that advantage or benefit is no different from competition, because it is the only inducement for purchasing the product, *emphasize* it in specific terms. Whatever the type of headline, and no matter to whom it is addressed, it should as dramatically and as vividly as possible acquaint the reader with what the entire advertisement has to say. In short, it should make clear "what's in it for him or her." A number of textbooks classify headlines by "types" — by which is meant particular structure. Greyhound's famous slogan (which may have originally been a headline) *Take the bus and leave the driving to us* has been termed "directive." It might also have been called "imperative" since it gives a command. Headlines that state what a product or a service will do for the reader that might prove beneficial are frequently referred to as "direct benefit" headlines. Headlines that do not immediately reveal what it is they have been intended to convey are often incorrectly called "curiosity" headlines meaning, of course, "curiosity-provoking." However headlines are classified, a copywriter does not say, "I am now going to write a 'news' headline" or "a 'gimmick' headline" or "a 'hornblowing' headline." Generally a copywriter writes what comes to mind and seems most appropriate.

An overall admonition in the writing of effective headlines is to avoid general statements. Whatever is said in the headline should be specific and concrete. The abstract statement should be shunned. State in understandable language the benefits of the product and what the product will do for the reader or auditor.

QUESTIONS, SUBJECTS FOR DISCUSSION

1. What should a headline generally accomplish?

2. In what ways does it do this?

3. Is a clever use of words in a headline ever justifiable?

4. How long should a headline be?

5. How many readers read headlines in contrast to how many read copy?

6. What kinds of words are preferable to use not only in headlines but in copy? In writing a headline, what should the copywriter constantly keep in mind about what he or she is going to have it say to the reader?

7. Describe Korzybski's "structural differential" and give an example other than "cow."

PROJECT

Glance through a number of newspapers as well as of national magazines and:

1. Select those headlines which, in your opinion, tend to attract the target market for the product.

2. Select a similar number which fail to attract the target market.

3. Re-write the latter in a way that would say something about the product or service which would flag target readers and induce them to read the copy for additional information.

Cover a minimum of five headlines in each category and cite reasons why you have either selected or re-written them.

Chapter 14

Corporate Advertising – Magazines

Corporate advertising – which was once (and still is occasionally) called institutional advertising – is advertising undertaken to benefit the advertiser in ways other than through the purchase of a product or the use of a service, although it can and frequently does contribute to such purchase through the impression it creates of the company. Its objective may be to create a favorable "image" of the company. It can attempt to do this in a number of ways. For example, it can acquaint the audience of the medium carrying its message with company policy towards customers (its willingness to take back its product at any time if it does not give full satisfaction), towards employees (the fringe benefits it offers), and towards stockholders (its record of dividend payments). It can cite the concern of its management for the environment (steps taken at its plants to avoid pollution of the surrounding area, or public service advertising to contribute to the prevention of forest fires). It can cultivate confidence in its research and development program (examples of its technological achievements). It can win the support of conservatives by publishing messages on the advantages of free enterprise or of liberals by publishing messages on the importance of caring for the needy or eliminating poverty. These must be based, of course, on actual management attitudes.

In the event of a strike, the company can employ corporate advertising to gain support for its point of view in the dispute that caused the strike. If state, federal or local legislation is impending that would increase the company's costs, lower its profits or both, or interfere with the sale of its products (e.g., a tax on advertising), it can use corporate advertising not just to express its opposition to the passage of such legislation – giving its reasons, of course – but to enlist the backing and active support of the public.

Corporate advertising had its beginnings in the desire of successful owners of growing businesses to boast of their accomplishments. Almost invariably such advertising included drawings or photographs of the factory or of the founder or present owner of the business. Out of these naive beginnings grew a more astute use of corporate advertising, notably as the public became more sophisticated, as government intruded on business operation, and influence groups came into being (labor, minorities, agriculture) seeking protection or advantage through political means.

It is difficult to measure the effects of corporate advertising unless a specific communications objective is established and, in addition, unless research is undertaken both before and after the appearance of the advertising to determine the degree of change in attitude on the part of that segment of the population regarded as the target market.

Corporate advertising, thus, is one of the most difficult forms of advertising to write well. First of all, very few advertising copywriters have a sufficient awareness or knowledge of business to write it with assurance. Second, because writing is an "art," and because business executives generally are interested in more practical matters, an inimical attitude exists between business executives and writers. Actually this is and can prove to be to the benefit of each since it can provoke more searching questions on the part of the copywriter and more explicit explanations on the part of the business executive. Third, the public, by and large, does not find business interesting and, as a result, the copywriter must find ways to *inject* interest into what might otherwise be advertising "not worth reading." One effective way of doing this is to avoid the tendency of most advertising to be totally laudatory by the writer assuming that he or she is a newspaper reporter doing a factual story about the company or covering a vital aspect of its operation.

The interest in product advertising springs largely from interest in the product, what it does and how it looks so that most product advertising has an interest factor apart from that created by its design or the manner of its writing. It can, as a consequence, prove to be to some degree effective despite undistinguished, even poor, writing and design. Few businesses possess a similar, inherent interest factor primarily because they are essentially—as a functioning entity—intangible. They consist chiefly of human interrelationships involved in planning, risk-taking, judgment, initiative, and rivalry. These are impalpable and are, in a sense, almost non-existent by comparison with a product. It is the importance of their existence, the consequences of their existence, and the environment essential to their existence that corporate advertising attempts to make real and understandable.

At its most effective, corporate advertising has the impact of a major news story or of an exciting essay. It opens windows of the mind. It is moving. It is memorable. Corporate advertising, in short, is a form of advertising that requires consummate skill and most clearly comes into being through the closest possible relationship between a top corporate official and a sensitive writer.

Magazines are a highly effective medium for corporate advertising because they are selective, making it possible for particular audiences to be reached with a message intended to cover their particular interests. Special treatment is required when television is the medium, chiefly because of time limitations. If newspapers are employed the message is most effectively told in editorial style and design.

This question inevitably arises: must the copywriter be in total agreement with the particular point of view of company management? And the answer is, it would be preferable—in the interests of both—if the copywriter were not. Otherwise, the writer might overlook the importance of writing in such a way as to gain the clearest understanding of that point of view among readers who were *not* of the same persuasion—which is the fundamental purpose of the advertisement. The writer should, if possible, have a relatively neutral reaction to the management's point of view. For example, if the writer were totally against it and opposed to its general acceptance, he or she could not possibly write in such a way as to obtain a reasonable acceptance of it. Under the circumstances, he or she should refrain from writing because this would expose the client to less than a clear and impartial delineation of that point of view. Product advertising seldom imposes such a responsibility, unless the writer has incontrovertible evidence of the worthlessness of the product.

This, of course, does not alter the fact that magazines are an effective medium for corporate advertising because they are so selective. They are also a medium in which—unlike radio or television—subjects can be treated at length.

QUESTIONS, SUBJECTS FOR DISCUSSION

1. What are some of the purposes of corporate advertising?

2. What is a fairly effective way to invest corporate advertising with some degree of interest?

3. What is it advisable for a copywriter to do in order to be able to write intelligible if not interesting corporate advertising?

4. Why is it easier to make a product interesting than a company?

PROJECT

Find three corporate advertisements in magazines and do a paper of not more than 500 words in which you state your opinion of what each appears to be directed at accomplishing, how effective—or ineffective—you believe it to be in accomplishing the objective, and your reasons for so believing.

In addition, appraise its layout design and, if you think it can be improved, improve it, explaining why you re-did it as you did.

Chapter 15

Direct Response Advertising

Direct response advertising is related, as is catalogue advertising, to direct marketing: the transaction in selling and buying the product that is solely between manufacturer and individual purchaser. It is direct. No distributors, no wholesalers, no retailers are involved. The only intervening agent is the advertisement or the catalogue.

Direct response advertisements are easily recognized. They usually have an illustration of the product, a headline, copy of exceptional length, and a coupon or a phone number. Occasionally the advertiser will eliminate the coupon. As a result the reader — if he wants the product — will have to write a letter requesting it and enclose payment. A direct response advertisement without a coupon, however, is the exception — because, first, the coupon suggests and invites response and, second, it provides a way of responding that is convenient and less likely to cause mistakes of any kind since it is, in effect, an order blank that contains all required information and instructions, including price, shipping charges, and local taxes to be included, if any. Aside from these two easily recognizable elements — the coupon and the exceptional length of the copy — direct response advertisements have another distinguishing feature: a headline that emphasizes something unique about the product that is not available in similar products that are sold in retail stores. In fact, the product should *not* be available in stores. In direct response advertising, the most important element is the product, which must be or have some feature that is unusual.

It is not difficult to understand that if the product is not unique and is available at a nearby store, there is little compulsion to order by coupon. In terms of what is offered, when more than one product is advertised, coupon returns are invariably fewer — despite the greater number of items offered — than when the offer is confined to one product. Offering several items also complicates the coupon and makes filling it out difficult.

Indirect or "clever" headlines are seldom used in direct response advertising. This kind of advertising, which has one and only one opportunity to sell the product, is devoted totally to describing, in detail, features, advantages, and benefits of the product. The copy describing these features, advantages, and benefits is necessarily long for two reasons:

1. It must "sell" the product between the time the reader starts to read the advertisement and finishes reading it. All pertinent facts about the product *must* be given.

2. Because the headline is written to attract only individuals interested in the product, these individuals will want as much information as possible about the product in order to decide then and there whether or not to buy it.

The writer of direct response advertising must obtain many more facts about the product to be advertised than the writer of advertising intended only to build brand preference. Indeed, the more exotic and dramatic the information, the more interest in the product. Information such as source of origin, why that is important, what it contributes to the product's uniqueness and value, what the product will do that products similar to it will not do, and why it is priced as it is, either higher or lower than similar products, is important. In direct response, the more information given about the product, the more orders can be expected.

The coupon must be "framed" by a line of black dashes indicating that it is to be torn off or cut off the page and mailed. A line of dots framing it will be less likely to induce readers to cut it out and send it than a line of dashes. The dashes must be prominent — at least three points in thickness. The preferred position for the coupon is the lower right hand corner of the advertisement, or it can extend the width of the page. But never locate it elsewhere. On that score, coupon advertisements on right hand pages do better than those on left hand pages.

While the copy must be written to attract only those likely to be interested in the product — seldom 1 or 2 percent of the total circulation of the magazine — all the Starch principles known to promote reading of the copy should be employed. Short paragraphs. White space between paragraphs. Narrow measure columns. Subheads every two to three inches set in boldface, italic type. Type no smaller than nine point. Standard typefaces include: Garamond, Bodoni, Baskerville, Caslon. Serif type is preferable to sans serif type. Headline and subhead set in bold or demi-bold type, caps, and lower case. Descriptions must be as vivid and pictorial as possible. Generalities (as in all advertising copy) must be avoided. Select short, specific, concrete words. Keep sentences brief. Give plausible reasons for ordering immediately. Offer an advantage for sending the coupon by a certain date or with a check or money order enclosed — such as eliminating the shipping charge or offering a surprise gift.

Over the years, direct response or coupon advertising has had more practical research than any other type of advertising and any copywriter can learn much by reading as thoroughly as possible books written by authorities on the subject. In fact, many outstanding writers of general advertising have credited their experiences in writing direct response copy with the success they have had in writing all other forms of advertising. Certainly one lesson the writer of direct response advertising learns is the importance of the copy's telling as much as possible about the product, its value, and its worth. Copy not about the product or the reader has no place in direct response advertising — or, for that matter, in any kind of advertising.

Layout design for direct response advertising should be editorial in character — simple, unadorned, geometric in arrangement, and non-cluttered. Color is useful depending on the product. The product is usually shown prominently. The reader has no other way of determining its appearance.

One of the most helpful contributions to direct response advertising was the introduction by AT&T of the toll-free 800 number which has reached the point of out-distancing the coupon as a way of ordering the item advertised. The introduction of the credit card has also revolutionized direct response ordering, eliminating the writing of a check or obtaining a money order from the nearest post office. The 800 number is particularly useful for messages on TV or radio. Even in print advertising, it relieves the person responding of writing a check and, of course, of waiting for the check to be delivered by mail. As a consequence, most direct response advertisements in print media display an 800 number in boldface type.

QUESTIONS, SUBJECTS FOR DISCUSSION

1. What is meant by direct response advertising?

2. What are the two most distinguishing physical features of direct response advertising?

3. Why is response more likely with a coupon than without one?

4. What are the reasons for lengthy copy in a direct response advertisement?

5. What are the most important elements in a direct response advertisement? Why?

6. Why is a knowledge of how to write successful direct response advertising helpful in writing effective general advertising?

7. What have the 800 number and the credit card done for direct response advertising?

PROJECT

Read and analyze a number of direct response headlines. Then find a relatively unique product, such as a clock that has only hands and no face, or a foreign dictionary made of plastic that can be fanned open with one hand, or a tea set (pot, creamer, and sugar) that is the only bone china made in Ireland, and create a direct response advertisement of it.

TYPICAL TOTALLY FACTUAL
DIRECT RESPONSE HEADLINES

(For a fountain pen with a
light at the point)

For the active mind that never stops, even at 3 or 4 a.m.

THE NITE-WRITER PEN – LETS YOU JOT DOWN IDEAS

IN THE DARK AND GO RIGHT BACK TO SLEEP

No getting up to turn on a light	No waking or disturbing others	No stumbling in the dark to your desk

(For a product that causes rain
to blow off windshield)

Created by an aviator for safety in the sky

NOW RAIN-X, THE INVISIBLE WINDSHIELD WIPER,

ADDS TO YOUR SAFETY ON THE ROAD

At 35 mph, rain blows right off your windshield. So does
mudsplatter from trucks. One treatment good for 100 miles.

TYPICAL COUPON COPY
FOR A DIRECT RESPONSE ADVERTISEMENT

Name of company to which coupon is to be sent

Address

City, state, and zip code

Please send me ( ) Nite-Writer pen(s) at \$6.95 each. I enclose a check ( ) money order ( ) in the amount of \$_____ plus \$_____ for handling and shipping.

Or charge my AMEX ( ), VISA ( ), or Mastercard ( ) credit card No. _____ expiring _____. Include state tax.

Name _____

Address _____

City _____ State _____ Zip_____

For faster service, call toll free 1-800-000-0000 any time of day or night.

Chapter 16

Direct Mail Advertising

Direct Mail advertising used to include a number of types of advertising that came by mail and was also frequently referred to as mail order advertising. Today, however, it refers strictly to advertising that is delivered by the mail carrier and looks like mail. It is part of direct marketing and what was once the Direct Mail Association is now called the Direct Marketing Association because its interests include all forms of marketing that involve direct communication between advertiser and prospective customer. If for, example, you wish your name removed from all lists used by direct marketers you write a request to the Direct Marketing Association, Inc., at 6 East 43rd Street, New York, NY 10017.

Most direct mail advertising comes in standard No. 10 envelopes but could come in one that measures 3 1/2 by 6 1/2 or even 6 by 9 inches. Direct mail advertisers try to have their mailings look unique in order to attract the attention of the recipient. The "headline" of a direct mail piece is a statement printed on the envelope, usually along the bottom under and to the left of the address. Its purpose is the same as that of the headline of a print advertisement on the opening line of a broadcast commercial—to flag the most likely prospects and to interest them in opening the envelope to read the contents. As with any headline, the closer it is to the recipient's interest and the more genuine and helpful it sounds, the more effective it will be in inducing the reader at least to look at the contents of the mailing.

Obviously, unless the contents are inspected and read, the objective of the mailing—to have the reader order whatever is offered— **will not be achieved. In this respect it must be emphasized that the** more a direct mail piece resembles an actual letter, the more likely it is to be of interest. Letters sent bulk rate or addressed to *Occupant* or *Resident* are immediately recognizable as what is generally referred to today as "junk mail" and treated as such. It is more expensive to use an actual stamp and to address the mailing to an actual individual but the true cost of any advertising must be determined by the results obtained, not simply by the number of people reached.

In selecting any advertising medium the primary objective is to cover, per dollar spent, as much of the target market — or actual prospects for the product — as possible. In this respect, no medium is more selective than direct mail because actual lists and addresses of people that comprise the target market can be obtained. It is, however, useless to reach these people with a message that fails to interest them in the product. In any direct mailing, however, the quality of the list is vital in obtaining a sizable response.

One final word about lists. The most effective lists to obtain are those containing names of people who have responded to direct mailings within the past three to six months. Despite the highly selective nature of lists — in terms of occupations, incomes, life-styles, and so on — among these highly desirable individuals there are those who actually prefer to shop and order by mail, and these, obviously, will be more likely to respond to your offer than those who have responded less recently or frequently.

Because what is sent is a mailing, the most important piece to be extracted from the envelope should be a letter personally addressed to the recipient. It should waste no time in explaining why it has been sent and making clear what benefits are to be obtained by responding. Following Starch principles, the paragraphs should not be too lengthy. They should, however, stick to the subject and, by so doing, show respect for the reader's time. Included with the letter should be a leaflet providing more information about the product and any technical details that would be inappropriate to include in a letter. The leaflet should be kept uncluttered and the cover should contain a simple headline that invites opening and reading of the contents. To make it as easy as possible for the recipient to respond, an order form should be included that is not difficult to fill out and which contains all instructions essential to ordering, including an 800 number to call to induce more immediate response. If responses by mail as well are expected, they can be increased in number by the inclusion of a self-addressed, stamped envelope. Many direct mail advertisers have found that the inclusion of a "P.S." —on the letter or on a separate piece of paper—the major purpose of which is to give those who were almost ready to respond but decided not to, still another reason for responding—is a highly effective way to increase response.

It is helpful in any kind of advertising for the writer to write as if addressing a friend whose attention he or she wishes to call to a product and to the benefits that friend may expect from the product. It cannot be said too many times that too much advertising appears to those who read it or hear it as if they were seen by the advertiser as prey or victims. The writer should keep in mind that any direct mail advertising will probably arrive together with personal mail and the more helpful and friendly the manner in which it is written, the more likely it will be read and responded to. There are few products that do not have some advantage which justifies their being called to attention. As a result, the writer should not feel that, in writing the advertisement in a friendly manner, he or she is in any way being artful or deceitful. The exchange of products or services is the means by which all of us manage to sustain ourselves and the exchange of information about the merits or faults of the products we buy or the services we retain are common subjects of conversation. Such conversation, as a matter of fact, has been called the most effective and least expensive kind of advertising—word-of-mouth, as it is usually referred to. The advertising you write should be written to stimulate additional word-of-mouth advertising about its subject, just as genuinely informative articles in magazines stimulate discussion of the subjects they cover. This applies to all kinds of advertising, but especially to direct mail.

QUESTIONS, SUBJECTS FOR DISCUSSION

1. What, specifically, is considered direct mail advertising?

2. Why can direct mail advertising be called the most personal kind of advertising?

3. What is the "headline" of a direct mail piece and where is it generally found?

4. Describe the contents of a properly done direct mailing.

5. What two factors contribute most to the response from a direct mailing?

6. What other factors contribute to response aside from effectively written copy?

7. What are the most effective kinds of lists to use?

PROJECT

Obtain from a relative, friend, or neighbor — or from your own mail — a direct mail piece recently received. Analyze it. Determine ways that it could have been improved. Improve it by re-writing it and give your reasons why you think you have improved it.

Chapter 17

Trade Advertising

Most consumer magazines have as their purpose and reason for being the provision of useful and helpful information, not entertainment. By contrast, trade magazines are edited and published to provide specialized information to individuals as owners, managers, or employees of businesses engaged in the sale of products that consumers use. Advertising in consumer magazines attempts to persuade readers to purchase particular products or services for personal convenience, gratification, or enjoyment. Advertising in trade magazines attempts to persuade people engaged in business to invest in products for sale to customers.

Advertising to consumers has as its aim the purchase and use of merchandise in strictly limited quantity—a bottle or a six-pack of a cola beverage, several bars of soap, a carpet, a suite of furniture, an automobile. Advertising to retailers has as its goal the purchase of cases of cola, soap by the dozens of bars, carpets in large quantities, suites of furniture, and automobiles not for personal gratification but for operating a business or earning a living. The nature of trade advertising, therefore, is considerably more factual and practically informative than advertising addressed to consumers. It must be, because if retailers are to be persuaded to spend hundreds or thousands of dollars to stock a given product, they must be convinced that what they buy will sell. Under the circumstances, the retailer requires evidence that there is a market for the product, that for the amount of space devoted to its storage and/or display, he or she can anticipate a profitable return. The retailer is interested in what the manufacturer has done and is doing to stimulate demand for the product, the kind and amount of advertising scheduled to promote purchase, the nature of the point of sale material available, and the incentives offered (if any) to stock and "push" the product in preference to a competitor's product.

Because an advertising agency's commission on trade advertising is small in comparison with the commission it enjoys from the purchase of space in consumer media, there is an understandable tendency on the part of advertising agency management to assign the writing of trade advertising to lower paid and less experienced copywriters. Yet trade advertising requires considerably more knowledge on the part of the copywriter than consumer advertising does. In addition, even when seasoned copywriters are given trade advertising to write, they still may not be as well acquainted with the particular trade with which the product is associated or be as familiar with its jargon as they should be.

It is strongly advisable, for copywriters assigned the writing of a trade campaign, to read thoroughly the trade magazines in which their advertising will appear, the editorial material, and the advertising the magazines carry. In addition, they not only should be permitted by their employer but urged to visit retail outlets at which the product is or will be sold to ask questions of the managers of such outlets as well as the salespeople in them. No more effective way exists to gain the knowledge and familiarity required to write plausible trade advertising.

Retailers subscribe to trade magazines, as consumers buy magazines *they* read, primarily for the editorial content—which, in trade magazines, is a continuing manual of instruction in how to improve sales. Obviously if the advertising to appear in these magazines is to be of prime interest to the retailer it should be similarly instructive. Humorous or clever comments should be avoided unless through their humor or catchy phrasing they convey forcibly what the retailer is most interested in getting—usable, business-building counsel and advice. The trade press is not read for entertainment. It is read for the same purpose that a textbook is read—for instruction in how to perform more effectively a given activity.

In trade copy, even more than in consumer copy, generalities, broad statements, and promises must be avoided, "Boost sales" . . . "increase profits" . . . "build store traffic" . . . such broad statements are all too commonly encountered in trade magazine advertising. If they are to be made and, more important, if they are to be taken seriously, they must be specific — "Boost sales 25 percent" . . . "Increase profits 50 percent" . . . "Build store traffic 1 1/2 times its present volume." And, of course, such statements must be backed by evidence that they can be attained. This is usually done by citing the experience of retailers who have employed the promotions or displays by which the gains stated have been achieved. In order for these examples to be accepted as having actually occurred, they should carry the name and location of the retailer and the retail outlet at which they were experienced.

Finally, a copywriter should write trade advertising only after he or she is satisfied that the copy will not be questioned by the retailers who read it as having all too obviously been written by someone who is not thoroughly acquainted with the business. To avoid this, the writer should not only become as familiar as possible with the trade and its practices — which can never be quite as thorough as that of retailers who have spent most of their lives in the business — but should also expose the copy to actual retailers for their reactions to it.

QUESTIONS, SUBJECTS FOR DISCUSSION

1. In what principal way does trade advertising differ from consumer advertising? Give examples.

2. Why must trade advertising be specific in its statements?

3. What is advisable for a copywriter to do before attempting to write trade advertising?

4. Why is this helpful?

5. **What one final step** is advisable before a trade advertisement is released for publication?

PROJECT

Find three trade advertisements, each in a different field. Explain what you think they are attempting to do and whether or not you believe they are doing it well. If you feel any one of them can be improved in both writing and design, explain why you think so and re-do each as you think it should have been done. If you have time, see several retailers in fields to which the advertisements are directed and ask their opinion of your re-do's.

Chapter 18

Industrial Advertising

Industrial advertising has a limited and highly selective audience. Unlike the broad and general audience for consumer advertising, the audience for industrial advertising is comprised of individuals in managerial positions in companies manufacturing a broad diversity of products, most of them not intended for end use. In fact, few industrial products — from cotter pins to steel I-beams — are considered by users of the end product to have been made by companies other than the company manufacturing the end product.

The springs in a sofa are not necessarily made by the company that assembles the sofa. The flavor in a gelatine dessert, the scent in a perfume, seldom come from the company whose name appears on either product. The steel in an automobile may come from a steel mill not owned by the manufacturer of the automobile. All these products, however, contribute importantly to the value of the end product of which they are a part — the sofa, the dessert, the perfume, the car.

Industrial products of all kinds exert an influence on the end product in terms of its price, its degree of quality, its durability, its preferability over similar competing products, its overall structure, and its performance. Because of this influence, the individuals responsible for the purchase decision on industrial products — engineers, chemists, purchasing directors, production managers, owners of small manufacturing businesses — are considerably more analytical in making their decision. They are also better qualified — in terms of education, training, and experience — to judge the value-contribution of the product they are solicited to purchase. And, of course, like retailers they do not spend a few cents or a few dollars when they buy — they spend hundreds, thousands, frequently hundreds of thousands of dollars. In addition, the industrial products they will purchase will, to varying degrees, affect not only the sales volume of the company employing them but its profit as well.

For all these reasons, the writer of industrial advertising—like the writer of trade advertising—must assemble many more facts and supporting evidence for the claims made than the writer of consumer advertising. The industrial advertiser must have a more thorough knowledge of the company that may use the product than a writer of consumer advertising need ever have about the consumer whose purchase he or she attempts to influence. That knowledge must extend beyond demographics. It must encompass a thorough awareness of the businesses whose executives—minor or major—will be addressed. This is seldom knowledge or experience that can be acquired in a short time. The industrial advertising copywriter, therefore, tends to be a specialist—as the advertising agencies that acquire industrial advertising accounts tend to specialize in industrial advertising. Almost never is a qualified writer of consumer advertising capable of writing effective industrial advertising or a qualified writer of industrial advertising capable of writing effective consumer advertising.

Despite the difference in dollar volume between consumer advertising and industrial advertising—brought about because of the difference in cost between consumer media, in which cost per page is relatively high, and industrial media, where it is relatively low—there is a greater need for qualified industrial advertising copywriters than there is for qualified writers of consumer advertising. The reason is, there is more of it. Because industrial advertising requires more specialized knowledge than consumer advertising, industrial advertising accounts tend to change advertising agencies with far less frequency than consumer accounts do and industrial advertising copywriters, therefore, despite lower salaries, enjoy greater job security.

Insofar as advertising design structure is concerned, advertisements for industrial products benefit from the same structural patterns that consumer advertising benefits from. A cluttered layout for an industrial advertisement will suffer the same lack of noting and reading that a cluttered consumer advertisement will suffer. It will also benefit in attracting and holding readers from the same design and typographic principles from which consumer advertisements benefit. And, of course, despite the wide use of technical terms in industrial advertising, the same need for simple words, short sentences, and clarity of expression exists. The basic problem is still one of communication.

Because of this, the same discrepancy exists between effective and ineffective industrial advertising as exists in consumer advertising. Not just the more knowledgeable but the more skilled writer will write the more inviting, the more convincing, and the more memorable industrial advertising. The techniques of presentation are usually employed in all kinds of advertising to convey evidence and support claims. Testimonials are used, again from well-known and respected companies concerning improvements in quality, costs, or performance achieved through the use of the product being advertised. Physical tests demonstrating the efficacy of the product are helpful. The number and distinction of the companies using the product together with examples of technological innovations achieved by the company manufacturing the product are also important. As with all advertising, the closer industrial advertising comes to resembling the editorial content of the medium in which it appears, the more likely it is to be read and to be productive. Because it is addressed by one business to another, industrial advertising is also called business-to-business advertising.

QUESTIONS, SUBJECTS FOR DISCUSSION

1. How does the audience for industrial advertising differ from the audience for consumer advertising?

2. How does an industrial product generally differ from a consumer product?

3. How well acquainted must an industrial advertising copywriter be not just with the business that manufactures the product but of the businesses that will use it — and why?

4. What is the one thing industrial advertising and consumer advertising have in common?

5. List some of the techniques of presentation that are fairly common to industrial advertising.

PROJECT

Obtain three industrial advertisements, each containing a different approach or way of demonstrating why the product advertised should be considered for purchase and use. Analyze each of the advertisements for (1) believability, explaining why you find it believable or do not and (2) use of correct design principles, re-doing the design if you think it can be improved.

Chapter 19

Creating Store Traffic

The majority of newspapers are published and distributed locally and their major service to readers is providing news of the community in which the readers live. Their major service to advertisers is as a vehicle for information which attracts potential customers to stores in the locality. This is the prime advantage local media have over national media — they not only can serve as a source of data for buying, they can direct people interested in buying the products advertised to the stores in which those items are available and waiting for purchase. National magazines — unless they have local editions — and network television are limited to advertising that may create interest in a product but cannot always inform the reader exactly what its price is or where it can be bought.

Price and location are practical bits of information but they are useless unless in some way readers are induced to find the price attractive and to decide to purchase the item advertised. There are two basic kinds of advertising which accomplish this and, in doing so, build store traffic. The first of these is sale advertising. The most attention-compelling and interest-arousing word in a sale advertisement is the word SALE — which should always be featured and set in larger type than any other information in the advertisement. Next in importance is what is on sale and, in relation to that, the price to which it has been reduced and the amount of the saving the reduction makes possible. The formula for this is usually *Was — Is Now — You Save*, with the appropriate figures. The saving can be either in actual dollars saved or in the percentage of the saving in relation to the original price.

Once it has been established that a sale is being held, what is on sale, the price at which it is being offered, and the amount of saving this makes possible, the advertisement should state when the sale begins and, no less important, when it ends. There are two obvious reasons for this. The first is to enable the reader to decide when to visit the place at which the sale is being held and the second is to induce the reader to go promptly by establishing a time limit. The inducement to go promptly is frequently intensified by announcing a limit on the quantity of whatever is on sale. The phrase *Limited Quantity* is so general and has been used so frequently it is more effective if the quantity is specified. The second reason for establishing the time limit is to avoid having people arrive after termination of the sale and insist on being given the item advertised at the price at which it was advertised because the advertisement did not indicate when the sale would end. It is, of course, also essential to state where the sale is being held, if it is being held in a large store, and at what location in the store it can be found. Also helpful, in addition to mentioning the original price, is establishing the quality or reputability of the item on sale—by mentioning its brand name (if that is well known) or in some way establishing its worth and reliability. Unless this is established the saving will lack the degree of interest it necessarily has when the item offered is of recognizable worth.

The other type of advertising that builds store traffic is so-called image advertising for a store that creates a reputation of a particular kind that, in turn, attracts people interested in patronizing such a store. The reputation can be for quality merchandise. It can be for the store's standing behind the merchandise it offers by taking it back without question if it is found unsatisfactory. It can be for selling reliable merchandise at favorable prices. It can also be for having a broad selection of items in a particular category. Whatever the reputation, it not only attracts a certain kind of customer but helps set the store apart from its competition. This is advertising that reflects store policy. In many ways it is similar to advertising in national magazines directed at creating brand preference among products. Obviously the store competes with other stores offering the same kind of merchandise and, in this respect, is a "product." The advertising it runs to create reputation does so, not by claiming in so many words that the store deals only in quality merchandise, but by reflecting this in its tone, its appearance, in the kind of art work it employs, and in its typography. A store (or a product) is not unlike a human being in this respect — how it conducts itself in all its activities creates an impression that ultimately endows it with a reputation by which it is judged.

A store can speed the building of a reputation by running specific image-building advertising, a campaign of advertisements that have no other purpose than to create an impression. Their appearance must be regular and continuing. If an appropriate slogan can be created it can prove highly effective in causing potential customers to think of the store in a particular way.

Sale advertising creates immediate traffic. Image-building advertising creates it more slowly, but more steadily, and adds to the impact and interest of the store's sale advertising. Image-building advertising obviously is more effective than sale advertising in fostering customer loyalty and builds a sound defense against the possible inroads of competition. Sale advertising, in addition to creating immediate traffic and increasing highly desirable cash flow, can also introduce new customers to the store who, if they are aware of its reputation and find it justified by what they encounter on their visit, may just possibly continue patronizing it. Both types of advertising are essential to continued store growth.

QUESTIONS, SUBJECTS FOR DISCUSSION

1. Has newspaper advertising any advantage over national advertising and, if so, in what way or ways?

2. What basic elements of information should a sale ad contain?

3. What is the purpose of each of these?

4. Why is the phrase *Limited Quantity* not as effective in attracting people to a sale as specifying the actual number of items on sale?

5. What is the formula for establishing whether a sale is or is not **worth attending**?

6. What additional factor can make the sale especially attractive?

7. In what ways can image-building advertising contribute to the establishment of a particular reputation for the store?

8. What advertising device is useful in building reputation?

9. How do sale advertising and image-building advertising interact in contributing to store growth?

PROJECT

Visit a store in the community. Talk to its advertising manager to learn the reputation it is attempting to create. Determine for yourself whether or not the advertising it is running is accomplishing this as effectively as it might. Create your own image-building advertisement for the store as well as a sale advertisement for it, then show it to the advertising manager and get his comments.

Chapter 20

Sales Promotion

Sales promotion for many years meant activity primarily at point of sale to remind shoppers of the presence of products they had been acquainted with through advertising but may not have included on their shopping list or might have forgotten. It consisted chiefly of display material—window posters, counter cards, so-called shelf talkers, light hangs (or signs hung from light cords), end of aisle displays, and dump bins. Retailers originally were encouraged to employ display material to increase sale of the products featured on it and so increase "profits" for themselves; then, as products proliferated together with display materials, retailers were offered incentives, including free goods or cash, to use them. Despite changes in sales promotion activities over the years, its essential purpose remains the same—to induce retailers to stock a product, to move that product as promptly as possible, and in as large a volume as possible out of the retail outlet.

With inflation and, later, recession reducing product purchase, sales promotion attained a high state of sophistication in ways and means of inducing consumers to buy. It became known as "push" strategy as opposed to the "pull" strategy of advertising—"pushing" products towards potential customers after advertising had "pulled" them into the store. Various devices by which consumers could purchase products for less than the established price became the principal arsenal of sales promotion—cents-off coupons, 2-for-1 sales, premiums, special combinations of products, sales of various kinds tied in with holidays or other events, and refund deals. Such promotions are generally of short duration and for the sole purpose of inducing immediate purchase. Traditionally, major marketers spent, on the average, approximately 40 cents of every marketing dollar for sales promotion and 60 cents for advertising. Sales are more predictable with sales promotion than with advertising. At the same time, the brand preference that advertising creates adds to the effectiveness of the promotions because a bargain becomes a bargain only when the product on which a lower price is offered is of known and accepted quality. Even when more dollars are spent on sales promotion than on advertising, advertising remains an essential contributor to sales promotion and cannot be cut too far or eliminated altogether, or sales promotion loses its primary appeal.

Advertising is also the most efficient way of calling consumers' attention to whatever promotions are undertaken. Newspaper advertising became the most effective means of getting coupons of various kinds into the hands of potential users. While national magazines are also employed in various promotions in which coupons are offered for redemption, they do not have the extent of local coverage or offer the immediacy of newspapers. Newspapers also have the added psychological advantage of being seen as repositories of current happenings and being purchased for the details involved in those happenings. In a sense, promotions—especially when they are built around the possibility of purchasing a wanted and usable product for less than its established price—are news, and advertisements announcing them have an undeniable news value. Readers are inescapably drawn to them and read them for the details involved.

As a consequence, such advertisements should be treated as a source of news and the important details, the monetary saving and the manner in which this comes about, should be featured prominently. Such messages are not unlike advertisements featuring a sale—the opportunity should be stated, the saving made possible, the time for taking advantage of the offer and, of course, where the opportunity can be realized.

Promotions featuring incentives to purchase within a given time have an undeniable appeal to consumers together with an undeniable benefit (or benefits) to the company offering them. People in general welcome opportunities to save money and this opportunity, together with the extent of the saving, enables the company to move merchandise that might otherwise not move as promptly. While the company enables the consumer to benefit from buying "now," the many economic factors involved, such as the increase in cash flow, the opportunity to replace the depleted merchandise, and the introduction of the product to individuals who have not previously purchased it, more than compensate for the cost of the promotion. It is a situation in which both the purchaser and the seller benefit.

While it is next to impossible to predict the amount of merchandise brand advertising influences, sales promotions are generally predictable. There is a pattern in human behavior which contributes to this predictability. For example, if a price refund offer, used not only to promote immediate purchase but to attract purchasers of competitive products, were to be taken advantage of by every customer induced to purchase as a result of it, the company offering it would lose money. However, the general experience in price refund offers, involving sending proof of purchase to the manufacturer for the refund, is that only from 10 to 50 percent at the most of purchasers intending to obtain the refund ever go to the trouble of obtaining it. This does not make the offer false or illusory. It is what happens and an advertiser, aware of what happens, can safely make the offer.

Because of the predictability of human behavior and reaction, "two for the price of one" offers have advantages for the advertiser that half-price offers lack. In the half-price offer, the established price of the product is reduced and once the established price is reduced, it is usually difficult to have users of the product ever again satisfied with the normal price. In the "two for the price of one" offer the established price is maintained and the presumed "loss" to the manufacturer is actually the cost of producing the products. "Free" offers, it should be pointed out, can be made only when what is offered is in fact actually given away. If any conditions are involved they must, by law, be stated.

Other forms of sales promotion include contests and sweepstakes. As in advertisements featuring price saving, advertisements featuring contests and sweepstakes should be devoted chiefly to inducing consumers to enter the contest or the sweepstakes, not to promoting the product. Advertising that calls attention to any kind of sales promotion should be factual, detailed, and confined to informing consumers of the opportunity being offered and what is involved in realizing the opportunity.

FIFTEEN BASIC TYPES OF SALES PROMOTION

1. *Price* – sale, cents-off offer

2. *Special event* – with or without a price incentive

3. *Free merchandise* – one free with two purchased

4. *Promotional goods* – special sizes to induce trial

5. *Coupons* – in-ad, use on the next purchase (bounce-back), store redeemable, mail-in refund

6. *Contests* – (occasionally requiring purchase to enter) game involving skill, 25 words, limerick, naming new product, etc.

7. *Sweepstakes* – large prizes offered on chance basis with no purchase required

8. *Premiums* – on-pack, in-pack, sent-for, self-liquidating, etc.

9. *Tie-in offer* – combination of two or more brands, of same company or with another company

10. *Special packaging* – for greater utility or for re-use

11. *Combined purchase* – reduced price on purchase of another item

12. *Third party beneficiary* – favorite charity, plant a tree, Olympics, etc.

13. *Sampling* – actual product, smaller size or miniature offered free or at steeply reduced price

14. *Stamps* – S&H, Gold Bond, or company stamp (generally offered with frequently purchased items)

15. *Foreign carrier* – on-pack coupons for other types of merchandise, on-pack sample, or another item

QUESTIONS, SUBJECTS FOR DISCUSSION

1. What is the essential purpose of sales promotion?

2. What is the difference in strategy between advertising and sales promotion?

3. In what ways does advertising contribute to the effectiveness of sales promotion?

4. What is the most effective medium for acquainting consumers with local sales promotions and why?

5. In what way is a "two for the price of one" offer preferable to a half-price offer?

6. In what ways is advertising announcing a sales promotion opportunity similar to advertising announcing a sale?

7. Are there any restrictions to the making of an offer of free merchandise?

PROJECT

Find three advertisements announcing a sales promotion, explain the type of promotion involved and give your opinion of how effectively the advertisement creates interest in the promotion.

Chapter 21

Corporate Advertising — Newspapers

As cannot be stated too many times, people buy particular media for their editorial, not for their advertising content — and, as a consequence, advertising that is as helpfully informative as the editorial content is more likely to gain attention and be read than advertising that is not. Even when intended for magazines, corporate advertising that is written as if a reporter were doing a story about the corporation will inescapably be more readable and be taken more seriously than when it is all too obviously an advertisement. This applies even more strongly when the advertisement is to be published in newspapers. All corporate advertising has a point to make, which is why it is written and published. However, of all categories of advertising, corporate advertising remains the most inscrutable. It is generally laden with business and technical jargon which, even when decoded, is of *little* interest to the reader. It usually boasts of corporate accomplishments, but seldom relates benefits of those accomplishments to the reader who asks the same question that readers ask of advertisements for products: *What's in it for me?*

Headlines of corporate advertising tend to be vague and general and impart little meaning even when the copy is read. Mere curiosity about the meaning of a headline has little effect in getting the copy read. In fact, one of the three major purposes of a headline is to induce reading of the copy to obtain more facts than can be included in the headlines. As has been stated, six times as many people, on the average, read headlines as read copy. As a consequence, the headline of an advertisement, like a newspaper headline, should convey the essence of what follows in the copy — and, if the copy is not read, the headline leaves the reader with at least some idea of what is in the copy.

An advertisement for Rolm Corporation, a producer of computer-controlled business telephone systems, employed a headline reading THE MOVE IS ON. It takes little thought to conclude that this headline in no way promotes reading of the copy and leaves the scanner with no conception of the advertising message or, for that matter, of Rolm Corporation. A corporate advertisement for Sperry contained the headline WHEN YOUR FORTUNES DEPEND ON SEEING THE FUTURE, YOU'D BETTER KNOW HOW TO LISTEN. A justifiable interpretation of this headline would be that Sperry has created a talking crystal ball. From the same issue of *Business Week* in which these two advertisements appeared, an announcement of the merger of two southern railways carried the headline, FROM THE CHAMPIONSHIP HERITAGE OF TWO GREAT RAILWAYS COMES NORFOLK SOUTHERN CORPORATION – THE THOROUGHBRED. It is difficult to understand why corporations, when their managements wish to say something of interest, say nothing of interest and, instead, spout platitudes in stained glass attitudes.

Sperry did little better in saying what it meant in a newspaper, where news is the order of the day. Sperry's headline on a corporate advertisement in *The Wall Street Journal* was LISTEN TO THE SOUND OF A STRATEGY IN THE MAKING. In the same issue of the *Journal*, Toshiba Corporation used the headline, FLEXIBILITY IS THE MARK OF A WINNER. In another issue of the *Journal*, Kerosun, Inc. published a message from its chairman with the headline, AMERICAN CONSUMERS KNOW A GOOD PRODUCT WHEN THEY SEE IT. Corporate advertising, wherever it appears, if it is to be a sound investment in communication, must be of interest to the audience and to do so must carry headlines that unmistakably say something of personal import – such as the headline of an advertisement for the Puerto Rico Economic Development Administration in *The Wall Street Journal* which read, YOUR PAYROLL DOLLARS ARE 50% MORE PRODUCTIVE IN PUERTO RICO THAN THE TOTAL U.S. AVERAGE. Such headlines excite interest, not simply curiosity. The Puerto Rico advertisement was without a question a news headline in a newspaper.

There are many reasons, of course, why corporate advertising is as tedious and overblown as it is. One of these is that few copywriters know much about business. And because they do not, they tend to write largely what they are instructed to write by business management and to use the very words that business management employs in conveying what it wishes to say. To be able to write clearly and understandably about business, a copywriter should regularly read the business sections of newspapers and news magazines such as, *The New York Times* and *The Wall Street Journal*. Reading publications such as these will also help a copywriter better understand the economy in which advertising functions and the influence of the economy on production and consumption, the latter of which advertising is employed to stimulate. Doing so will also enable the copywriter to feel more at ease and to talk more intelligently with advertisers for whose products he or she writes advertising messages.

To be an effective copywriter, an individual must familiarize himself or herself with many businesses and how they function and what they contribute. Such knowledge not only enables the copywriter to create interesting corporate messages, it also enables him or her to write more persuasively trade advertising addressed to retailers and to cope more successfully with industrial or so-called "business to business" advertising. There are too few copywriters sufficiently aware of business and business practices to create genuinely compelling corporate advertising in an era in which such advertising is growing in volume because of the need for a more widespread conception of corporate activities and their contribution to the general economy.

Corporate advertising usually attempts to convey the character as well as the characteristics of a company—and because these, to no small extent, reflect the character and the characteristics of management—occasionally corporate advertising can be totally unrelated to what the business does or produces and simply reflect what its management thinks. An outstanding example is the campaign that ran in *The Wall Street Journal* for many years for United Technologies, under the direction and signature of its chief executive, Harry Gray. Each advertisement consisted of a brief headline, a narrow column of text running from top to the bottom of the page, and a brief, final message in which a free copy of the advertisement was offered to anyone writing for it. *The Wall Street Journal* reported that United Technologies advertising appeared to be read by more of its readers than any other campaign running in its pages and received more requests for reprints than any other. In its way, and through the points of view it expressed, the campaign helped create a respect and admiration for the company and its management. This is a fundamental objective of just about every corporate campaign but which is rarely so successfully achieved.

QUESTIONS, SUBJECTS FOR DISCUSSION

1. Why are newspapers a very effective medium for corporate advertising?

2. In what ways does corporate advertising differ from consumer advertising?

3. Insofar as readers are concerned, in what way does corporate advertising confront a copywriter with the same basic problem consumer advertising does?

4. How is that problem best solved – in corporate advertising as well as consumer advertising?

5. In corporate advertising, what does a business have in common with a product in consumer advertising?

6. List some of the benefits a copywriter can obtain by reading news weeklies, business publications, tradepapers, and magazines devoted to business and industry reporting?

PROJECT

Find five corporate advertisements, determine where in the copy their fundamental purpose is expressed, state whether their headlines relate this purpose to the potential readers, and if you believe they do not, state why you believe they do not, and write headlines that do – with subheads if you think them necessary.

Chapter 22

The Leaflet

Leaflets, folders, pamphlets, booklets, and brochures have separate but interlocked definitions. A folder is presumably an unstitched booklet. Brochure, however, derives from the French *brocher* — to stitch. Leaflet is the simplest of the lot being defined as "a few sheets of printed matter." All, however, have one thing in common — they are distributed by hand or by mail or are left at trafficked locations for pick-up, and, of course, they are intended to be read. Not only to be read but to bring about a desired end. For very good reason Tom Paine was known as a pamphleteer — as is anyone who consistently dispenses folded printed matter directed at influencing the minds of readers.

To be of influence, of course, the pamphlet, leaflet, folder, booklet, or brochure must be read. If it is thrown away without being read, it suffers the fate of the flower born to blush unseen. The first aim of the pamphleteer — or the leaflet writer — must be to attract the attention and arouse the interest of the potential reader in the contents of the piece. This is accomplished in the same way — or ways — in which noting and reading are brought about for a magazine advertisement: by the design of the cover and by the nature of the headline. A simple, unadorned cover, either white or in a solid color, lending primary emphasis to the title or headline, is by and large the most effective way of obtaining inspection of the title. The more distractions on the cover, the less attention given the title. The title must, by what it says and how it says it, excite the interest of the reader in learning what the contents say. As with the headline of an advertisement, the title of even a simple leaflet must appeal to the personal interest of the individual who inspects it and do so with sufficient cogency to cause that individual to wish to read what appears beyond the cover. Exciting curiosity alone is not enough — the merely curious may not comprise the target audience to which the leaflet has been addressed. In this respect, it is not always advisable for the advertiser to write or to design the booklet. The advertiser is usually too close to the subject to be able to extract from it its essential interest to someone totally removed from it. The leaflet must treat the subject in sufficient length to provide the reader with every fact he or she must have to be converted to use, whatever it presents. The use of Starch principles can aid in promoting thorough reading of the message — narrow columns of type, text set in 10 or 12 point type, unfilled widows, space between paragraphs, the use of subheads, the occasional use of words or phrases in italics, and serif rather than sans serif type.

When the piece is sent by mail with an accompanying letter, the letter can, in addition to the title on the booklet cover, stimulate interest in the contents of the leaflet. Letters sent with leaflets for this purpose should be relatively short and should not divulge any of the facts contained in the booklet. Instead the letter should briefly promote what is to be gained from reading the leaflet. Folders and pamphlets are frequently sent with monthly bills to promote the purchase of other products. Many are provided for this purpose by manufacturers of the products featured in them. When they are, space is usually left on the back cover for the sender's imprint. Folders in four colors almost invariably obtain more attention and inspection than folders in black and white. Except for folders or brochures featuring fashions, photographs are generally more informative than drawings.

Except when made available on counters in retail outlets, folders, leaflets, and booklets are distributed, usually, by mail and are generally a vital part of direct mail advertising, containing more information than can or should be included in a letter. The personal touch of direct mail, however, should be confined to the letter. The message in the brochure should be simple, clear, and specifically informative. Since leaflets, folders, booklets, and so forth must be acted on at once, the information provided should include the purchase or rental price charged, whether the action desired is to have the recipient mail in an order, phone it in over an 800 number, or visit the retail outlet. Decisions to purchase are seldom made without awareness of price.

QUESTIONS, SUBJECTS FOR DISCUSSION

1. Learn at first hand, from a dictionary or a printer, the distinction among leaflets, folders, pamphlets, booklets, and brochures.
2. What must be the first aim of the writer of a leaflet or brochure?
3. How is this best accomplished?
4. Why must the title of a booklet excite more than the curiosity of the potential reader?
5. What Starch principles apply to the design of a leaflet?
6. What should be the sole purpose of a letter sent with a booklet?
7. Why should price be mentioned in a folder, leaflet, or booklet?

PROJECT

Obtain several leaflets, folders, booklets, and brochures. Determine their purpose and analyze them to conclude how well or how poorly they have been done. Re-write one of them you consider poorly done in order to have it more closely fulfill its purpose. If you have been unable to find an accompanying letter to re-write, write one that might be mailed with it.

Chapter 23

Outdoor Advertising

Outdoor advertising is considered print advertising largely because most of it comes into being on a printing press. However, outdoor advertising includes commercial messages including those flashed from a blimp, carried in banners behind airplanes, or "written" in the sky with smoke.

A principal characteristic of outdoor advertising is that it is primarily display advertising. It is observed and read at some distance from the individual whose attention it is designed to capture. Its message is usually brief. Its design varies widely but has as its aim visibility. Because of this, outdoor advertising — particularly in the United States — is seldom aesthetically pleasing in contrast, for example, with much of the outdoor advertising seen in France, beginning with the posters of Toulouse-Lautrec. As a consequence, there is a continuing attempt on the part of many groups to have legislation enacted against its use. The outdoor advertising industry has opposed this but has done little to overcome it through establishing standards of design for outdoor advertisers to practice. The major offenders are local users of the medium. National advertisers, because they have skilled and imaginative designers to call upon — chiefly in advertising agencies — tend to use outdoor advertising with considerable more regard for aesthetic values.

It has been pointed out that the consumer whom advertisers wish to reach with their message does not turn to the various media — magazines, newspapers, radio, and television — for the advertising messages they carry but for their editorial content; and that the closer the advertising comes to duplicating the nature of the editorial content, the more likely it is to be of interest and not to offend. In that context, the creator as well as the user of outdoor advertising must remain aware that the outdoor medium is the *out-of-doors* to which the public turns for various reasons — from visiting commercial areas to shop (where outdoor advertising is seldom found objectionable) to touring the countryside for visual pleasure (where outdoor advertising is invariably found objectionable). Indeed, outdoor advertising is one medium above all others where pleasant design and humorous or picturesque language is not only welcomed but more likely to be remembered and acted upon than posters poorly designed and written with little imagination. Rhetorical devices, alliteration, rhyme, even puns, have a place in outdoor advertising because of their greater memorability. Outdoor advertising in practically all its forms, including transit cards, stimulates attention for a few seconds only and therefore requires memorable treatment.

The most common form of outdoor advertising is the print board which is usually 30 feet wide by 12 feet in depth. For convenience in designing an outdoor poster on a layout pad, it can be drawn 15 inches in width by 6 inches in height. As Starch principles apply to the effective design of advertising intended for newspapers and magazines, so do they apply to the effective design of posters. Black type, in caps and lower case letters, against a white or yellow background, obtains greater reading than white type against a red or a blue or a brown background. Messages printed totally in capital letters should be avoided. Sans serif type, however, is as legible on a billboard and as easily read as serif type.

A billboard can contain as many as five elements — a headline, a brief copy message, an illustration, a likeness of the product, and the product name. If the headline conveys the copy message and contains the name of the product, obviously four of these elements can be eliminated. However, it is advisable to retain at least a likeness of the product, not only to register it on the mind of the viewer but to add weight and impact to the design. In this respect, billboard advertising can be quite effective in the introduction of a new product because it can show the product large and in full color. A logical medium to employ with outdoor advertising is radio on which an extended message can be broadcast to supplement the brief message required by all forms of outdoor advertising.

Actually outdoor advertising must include the window signs and displays as well as the in-store counter cards and shelf talkers of sales promotion, because these are seen when the consumer is "out of doors" away from the "indoor" media—newspapers, magazines, television, and radio. While, among these, radio is heard out of doors as well as indoors, it is *with* its listeners more intimately and for a longer period than any of the outdoor media. Of the outdoor media, transit cards have a longer span of attention chiefly because of the protracted periods of time that passengers occupy buses, street cars, subway trains and commuter trains. As a consequence, longer messages can be used on transit cards than on billboards or other outdoor posters. Billboards tend to have messages three to eight words in length. If the message to be told requires 12 or more words, it must be remembered that billboard postings consist of many boards in many places and are posted for 30-day periods. Consequently, a longer message will ultimately be read in its entirety in that time. Nevertheless, the writer is better advised to conceive of outdoor advertising as being seen briefly and therefore make it concise, clear and memorable verbally and visually.

Outdoor advertising along highways is best used for products or services of interest to people driving—gasoline or diesel fuel, oil, tires, beverages, candy, cigarettes, restaurants, motels, hotels, and camping sites. Outdoor advertising in urban areas is best used for products available there. Because many products are not always thought of when consumers write shopping lists or are not thought of in terms of brand names, outdoor advertising provides an excellent reminder source when employed near shopping malls or other commercial areas.

QUESTIONS, SUBJECTS FOR DISCUSSION

1. Name at least seven different forms of "outdoor" advertising.
2. Why is radio, which is listened to in cars, on beaches, and even while walking, not considered an outdoor as well as an indoor medium?
3. What is the principal characteristic of outdoor advertising?
4. What Starch principles apply to the design of outdoor advertising?

5. How many elements can a billboard contain? To how few can these be reduced and how?

6. What medium can be used effectively with outdoor advertising and why?

7. What is the most common size of a billboard? What is its proportion?

8. What is a convenient size in which to design a billboard on a layout pad?

9. For what period of time are most billboards posted?

10. What does this make possible?

PROJECT

Design a billboard using a product appropriate for posting along a highway. Design another using a product suitable for posting near a shopping mall.

Chapter 24

Broadcast Advertising

It has been estimated that people spend, on the average, as much time with the principal communications media — newspapers, magazines, radio, and television — as they do sleeping: eight hours and 32 minutes or approximately 1/3 of the day. Of this time, almost 90 percent is spent with the broadcast media — three hours and 18 minutes with radio, four hours and 17 minutes with television.

Unlike newspapers and magazines, to which people devote barely an hour combined, not only the time they spend with the broadcast media but the nature of the attention they give them differ sharply — as do their attitudes. The print media require their total attention — the broadcast media, notably radio, do not. In addition, the attention they give the broadcast media is given for a totally different purpose — primarily to be diverted, to be entertained. This imposes upon the copywriter a totally different approach to advertising. With the print media the audience intently seeks information; with the broadcast media the audience seeks escape. Even when the broadcast audience tunes to the news, it is sensitive to how it is prepared and by whom. It finds greater interest in the news as presented by certain newscasters than by others and even attributes to given newscasters greater believability in the news they convey. Television news programs differ widely in the ratings they earn — which has little to do with the news but a lot to do with its manner of presentation. The broadcast medium, to use a term, is essentially show business, especially television. This factor inescapably affects the reception of broadcast commercials and requires of their creators an awareness of the difference in the mind-set of the broadcast audience. The interest in what is presented is heightened or lessened largely by how it is presented. While this is true of the print media as well, the "how" in broadcast media is dependent on theatrical rather than on forensic or rhetorical skill. Anyone writing radio or television commercials will benefit from training and experience in plot development, in character delineation, and in the writing of believable dialogue. The writer should have an awareness of the dramatic. He or she is in a different metier from the purely literary. What is created is to be heard and seen rather than read. Inexperience and inexpertness are more immediately obvious. The writer must become the storyteller. It is similar to the difference between reading poetry and hearing it spoken. At the same time, when expertly spoken or seen, the commercial can have a power, an immediacy, almost impossible to obtain in print advertising.

While readers of print advertising are aware that what they see and read are not being seen or read by them alone, there is a sense of privacy in reading print advertising that is not felt in listening to broadcast advertising. As a consequence, there is less sensitivity in reading about certain very personal items — such as denture cleaners and adhesives, hemorrhoid ointments, feminine hygiene products — than there is in hearing about them on either radio or television. Consequently, in writing commercials about such products, the copywriter must exercise a restraint that is not always needed in writing print advertisements about them. The writer cannot treat them in the same manner as he or she would in print. Reference has been made to the importance of having advertising in a given medium reflect the nature of the medium. The broadcast media are entertainment media and it is virtually impossible to be entertaining about products intended for the alleviation of the many ills to which flesh is heir. The broadcast media, of course, are also news media and a commercial that provides information about a product that is useful can certainly be welcome, particularly if presented in a newslike manner. In this respect, the person giving the commercial and his or her voice, and the manner of delivery are of primary importance.

In preparing print advertising a copywriter should know something about layout design and typography, particularly about typefaces because typefaces have a personality which should accord with what is said. For example, Bodoni is more formal than Caslon. The copywriter should not only be familiar with typefaces and their particular personalities but should have a voice in their selection for the copy. Similarly, in broadcast advertising the writer should be aware of the importance of proper casting and the influence on what is said of appearance, personality, and voice of the individual speaking. Conscious of this, the writer should exercise some influence in casting for radio as well as for television commercials. An advertising message is more than simply words, particularly in broadcast media, and the language, no matter how well phrased, is, when spoken, either more or less impressive than the language itself. What is written to be spoken requires a totally different style from what is written to be read and the more practiced the copywriter is in both spoken and written English, the more effectively the message will be conveyed.

QUESTIONS, SUBJECTS FOR DISCUSSION

1. How much time do people spend with the broadcast media?

2. Why do they spend this much time?

3. Why is it more difficult to advertise on the broadcast media than in the print media?

4. Explain the difference in how a print advertisement conveys its message from how a broadcast commercial conveys its message.

5. Why is it that a poorly done broadcast message can have a more immediate response than a print message?

6. Why is it more difficult to advertise a personal item — such as a denture adhesive — on the broadcast media than in the print media?

7. What similarity exists between an effective sales person and an effective broadcast commercial?

PROJECT

Spend an hour listening to radio and an hour viewing television. Indicate which of the commercials were entertaining and held your interest and which failed to capture your interest at all — and explain why.

Chapter 25

Radio Advertising

Radio is the most ubiquitous of media. Ninety-nine percent of all homes have radios—with an average of five or six radio sets per home. Ninety-five percent of all automobiles are equipped with radios. Radio is also the most portable medium. It is carried by people on picnics, at the beach, even when simply walking

Radio was intially a medium of entertainment, but since the advent of television, radio has become largely a medium of diversion, of background sound. Radio is seldom listened to intently—it is simply heard. The one item to which it is consciously tuned is the weather. But even with the weather announcement, the listening time is brief.

There is no doubt that what is heard on radio makes some impression on the mind and the memory but to a large extent it is unconscious. Nevertheless, unlike television which is turned to for specific programs, radio *is* tuned to for specific *content*—country music, rock, middle of the road, classical music, talk (between announcer and listeners) and news. When tuning in the radio for specific content, listeners tune in particular stations rather than programs. As a consequence, radio stations rather than radio programs provide advertisers with types of audience. Radio is the one medium on which youth can be reached in extensive numbers. Radio is, as well, a local medium. It is used by national advertisers but for local coverage. In this respect, it competes with newspapers. Its major purpose—like that of newspapers—is usually to build store traffic for local merchants. Because radio is heard rather than listened to, radio commercials—more than any other form of advertising—must begin by "tapping the listener on the shoulder." They must divert the listener from whatever he or she is thinking or doing. Unlike the television viewer whose attention is focused on the tube, the radio listener's attention is focused elsewhere if, indeed, it is focused at all. The statement has been made that 83 percent of our impressions reach us through the sense of sight. We read magazines and newspapers. We see billboards. We view television. There is nothing to read or see or view on radio. Radio is heard — and must compete for our attention with all the other noises we hear and, above all, with the multitude of things we are looking at. Because its only means of getting attention is through the ear, it must gain listeners' attention by what is heard. This could be an unusual noise, a strain of familiar or pleasant music, a request for attention, a clearly heard statement of immediate and urgent or vital interest to the listener. Aside from "tapping the listener on the shoulder," the opening lines of a radio commercial — in this instance a dramatized commercial rather than an announcer speaking alone — must establish "where" the conversation is taking place and who the characters are. If the characters were, for example, Christopher Columbus and Queen Isabella in a skit publicizing a Columbus Day sale, the opening line should not simply be a woman's voice saying, "Now listen to me" but a woman's voice saying, "Now listen to me, Christopher Columbus," with a man's voice immediately responding, "Yes, Queen Isabella." The tyro, writing a radio commercial, all too frequently assumes that if the names Christopher Columbus and Queen Isabella appear on the typewritten script the audience will know what two people are talking. It may be equally useful to establish the time at which the conversation is supposedly taking place — with the Queen, for example, saying, "I know it's only 1492, but if Macy's is to have a Columbus Day sale on October 12 in 1992, you'd better get packing." Once the listener's attention is won, it must be retained. Whatever is done initially on the commercial to rouse the listener must be followed by a message whose content or delivery does not allow the interest to wane. There is another very compelling reason for this: it is extremely difficult for any human being to remember from one moment to another exactly what has been heard. It is equally difficult — and common — with radio commercials. How a radio commercial is written, therefore, is of vital importance. It is the contention of this volume that how any form of advertising is written marks the essential difference between outstanding and mediocre communication. In radio, however, the "how" also makes the difference between whether the message is listened to or is ignored.

In terms of holding and retaining interest, as well as having what is said remembered, the number of words employed also contributes. A 60-second radio commercial, if one person is speaking, can contain as many as 160 words. However, if the number is held to 130 or even fewer and the words, as a consequence, are spoken more slowly — with less content to be assimilated — it is easier for the listener to remember what was said.

Perhaps the major problem a radio commercial faces is that, to all too many copywriters, radio is not as "exciting" a medium to write for as television, magazines, newspapers, or even billboards. Few copywriters become prominent as a result of the radio commercials they have written despite the number of products that have become successful chiefly through radio. Of these, Pepsi-Cola must be first and foremost because of the famous jingle written by Allen Kent and composed by Ginger Johnson. Carolina Rice was another product built principally by radio in a jingle derived from the once popular song, *Nothing could be finer than to be in Carolina in the morning.* And until the advertising of Manischewitz wine was taken off posters and put on radio, countless people did not know how to pronounce its name in order to ask for it.

Radio should be one of the most exciting of advertising media to write for primarily because it does demand of a copywriter more thought and creative insight than the other media. When used for the right reasons and in the right way, radio is not only the equal of any other medium but when it makes the most of sound and hearing, it can prove superior. The enticement of television, its show business nature, and the degree of its impact on its audience have probably been the major reasons for the lack of competence and imagination that so large a number of its commercials exhibit. A television commercial does not provide the challenge that a radio commercial provides — or the degree of creativity. In a television commercial sheer physical production can compensate to some degree for poor writing. It cannot in a radio commercial.

HOW TO TYPE A RADIO COMMERCIAL

Name of Advertiser
Radio spot
30 seconds

YOUNG MAN: Rapunzel! Rapunzel!

RAPUNZEL (*heard from inside a stone room:* Just a minute. (*slight pause, then heard on open balcony*). Which one of you is it? Oh — Harry.

YOUNG MAN: Yes, Rapunzel, it is I, Harry. Let down thy golden hair so that I may climb to thy balcony.

RAPUNZEL: Harry, I've just been looking at my hair. I'm mortified. You should see the broken ends. Harry, this climbing my golden locks has got to stop.

YOUNG MAN: But, Rapunzel, I wish to be with thee!

RAPUNZEL: Sorry, Harry, I'm calling it quits. I got a date with Command Performance to see what they can do for my hair.

YOUNG MAN: Command Performance?

RAPUNZEL: It's a new hair cutting and styling salon at Kingston Four Shopping Plaza. Just opposite Rodgers Cadillac. Fourteen trained hair specialists. No waiting. And it's open Monday through Friday, ten to nine. Saturday, ten to seven.

YOUNG MAN: Then just for once, Rapunzel, before Command Performance separates us forever — let down thy golden locks!

RAPUNZEL: Harry — have you ever heard of a ladder?

WHAT TO KEEP IN MIND ABOUT RADIO

1. Seldom tuned in for itself. Usually heard while listener is doing something else. So — catch attention and hold interest.
2. No picture to get or hold attention — so use unusual statement or something of great personal interest to the target market.
3. Devices for catching and holding interest can be: use of well-

known personalities to deliver message, interviews, comedy, suspense, or sound effects.

4. Because of short attention span, use short words, and short sentences. Keep word count no longer than 160 for a 60-scecond spot — 150 for females. If conversation involving two or more people, use even fewer words to allow for pauses, etc.

5. Impress name of product and principal selling point or benefit — and repeat before close of commercial.

6. Write naturally. Avoid standard advertising phrases. Write so commercial sounds as if announcer is talking to a friend or an aquaintance.

7. Write, then edit. Read it aloud to yourself to avoid unfortunate liaisons between words or awkward phrasing.

8. If commercial is open end — or written to include a local announcement at end — allow ten seconds for this.

9. If you write a jingle, be certain it says something about the product and that, when sung, anybody listening can understand every word.

10. If commercial is for local use only, mention price and where product can be purchased. Perhaps include some local reference.

QUESTIONS, SUBJECTS FOR DISCUSSION

1. Why can radio be called "the most ubiquitous of media?"

2. In terms of consumer involvement, what distinguishes radio from the other major media?

3. Because radio is primarily local, what should be the major purpose of a radio commercial?

4. What is the first thing a radio commercial must do if its message is to be heard — and why?

5. Why must a dramatized radio commercial establish immedi-

ately who is speaking and, occasionally, where the conversation is taking place? Give an example.

6. What number of words is allowable in a 60-second commercial and why is it probably advisable to use fewer?

7. What opportunity does radio offer a copywriter?

PROJECT

Catch three radio commercials on a tape recorder, analyze them, state their purpose and how well they meet the requirements of a successful commercial—or how badly they fail. Then, re-do them in a way in which you believe they would be more effective.

Chapter 26

Radio Opportunities

As has been stated several times, the nature of any advertising is inescapably related to the nature of the medium in or on which it reaches its intended audience. This applies particularly to radio advertising. When print advertising is considered, the mind instantly visualizes a message conveyed by type or lettering on a spatial surface. As a consequence, design is of primary importance — whether the message appears on a newspaper page, a magazine page, in a leaflet, or on a billboard. When television advertising is contemplated, the mind conjures up pictures in motion, spoken words, and music. By contrast, when the mind thinks of radio advertising it can conceive only of sound — language, chiefly. This is a limiting factor in conceptualization because only one sense is involved — that of hearing, and hearing has less impact on consciousness than sight. Therefore, when writing for radio, copywriters must be constantly mindful of this and, in their written messages, use words and suggest sounds that are most likely to arouse attention and evoke interest. Many texts on radio copywriting advise the use of words that create pictures in the mind, and examples are cited such as Rupert Brooke's lines from *The Great Lover:*

> . . . the cool kindliness of sheets . . . the rough
> male kiss of blankets, The benison of hot water . . .

But the words used must accomplish more than the creation of pictures. They must create *interest* in what is being said. For example, there is probably no more effective way in which to begin a radio commercial for a cold remedy than, "If right now you are putting up as best you can with the miseries of a cold . . ." or to start a commercial to draw males into a department store to purchase clothing than, "This Saturday, Gimbel's is having a sale on men's clothing in which you can save from fifty to seventy-five percent on well-known brand name suits . . ." Like the headline on an advertisement, the opening statement in a radio commercial should single out the logical prospects for what the commercial is intended to sell and provide a compelling reason for those logical prospects to buy.

Indeed, it is advisable for anyone writing a radio commercial to write every line as if it were a headline and not to overburden the commercial with too many words for the mind to remember. It is more difficult for a human being to remember what is heard than what is read. Hence the advisability of using clever phrases and statements, humor, rhyme, alliteration, other rhetorical devices and, of course, song.

As pointed out in reference to the radio commercials that helped build acceptance for Pepsi Cola, for Carolina Rice, and for Manischewitz Wine, radio is an excellent medium for establishing the names of new products—when done in a way that makes greatest impact on the mind. In two of these instances this was accomplished through memorable jingles and in the third by telling potential purchasers how to pronounce properly a name which, in print, could be assumed to have at least three possible pronunciations. Jingles—or singing commercials—are a highly useful way in which to register on the mind not only product or store names but features of products or services of stores. In doing this, however, the dependence of radio on sound alone must cause the creator of a singing commercial to keep the jingle simple and easy to understand and the music sufficiently melodic to implant itself in the memory. David Ogilvy has been quoted as saying that if a door-to-door sales representative sang to the individual who answered the door the representative would have more doors closed in his or her face than by just speaking. But a radio commercial is not a door-to-door sales representative. It is an electronically delivered message. Mnemonic devices are advisable as well as voices that are distinctive, welcome, and have a human rather than a mechanical quality to them. Voices that tend to sound uninterested in what they are saying and speak all too obviously because they are being paid to do it will not suffice. For this reason, it is also extremely effective to have the message delivered by a well-known, respected, and popular personality. It adds a quality of interest that an impersonally delivered message lacks. This applies as well to having a jingle sung by a personality rather than by someone who cannot be visualized.

The integrated radio commercial, that is delivered as part of the program or by the principal performer, usually obtains a greater degree of audience response than the commercial delivered during an interruption in the program or at the beginning or end of the program by a station announcer. Whether this is because it elicits more attention or because the performer provides greater empathy has never been determined. However, on programs soliciting mail or phone response, the response is regularly higher when the commercial is more directly associated with the program or with one of its participants than when it is identified only with the advertiser.

This emphasizes the importance of creativity in the writing as well as in the staging of the commercial, the contribution to overall effectiveness by *how* what is said is said. Advertisers almost invariably are more concerned with *what* is said about the product than with *how* it is said. Commercials, however, are not unlike company sales representatives in this respect — provided with the same facts, the sales representative with a winning personality will prove more effective than the sales representative without a winning personality. This, of course, is true of all advertising but is especially true of radio advertising — confined as it is to reaching the audience through only one of the senses — hearing.

All media offer opportunities for new, fresh, and more vigorous use by advertisers. Radio has had all too little of this. Its commercial use was considerably more imaginative when its programming was also more imaginative, when radio carried programs such as television carries today, comedy programs, dramatic programs, musical programs. Today stations have become stereotyped — only one type of program is provided and that one endlessly without variation. Radio is the one medium that provides advertisers with round-the-clock listening. If its material were fresher, and more varied, radio listening might not be as apathetic as it is. Commercials might be brighter and less stereotyped than they are. Sound effects might be used more liberally than they are — in both station programming and advertising commercials. Radio is a medium that needs and merits more thought regarding its use.

QUESTIONS, TOPICS FOR DISCUSSION

1. When writing a radio commercial, of what limiting factor in communication should the copywriter be aware? And why?

2. Being aware of this limiting factor in the communication of the message, how should the copywriter attempt to overcome it?

3. In what ways does the opening statement of a radio commercial resemble the headline of a print advertisement?

4. What are some of the mnemonic devices the writer of a radio commercial can use?

5. What advantages does the voice of a respected or popular personality have over that of a station announcer?

6. In what ways can radio commercials be integrated with the program during which they are heard?

7. What is the major contribution of creativity in the writing and use of a commercial?

PROJECT

Listen to and appraise several radio commercials, some of which attempt to induce people to buy a product, the others of which attempt to induce listeners to visit a particular store. Among those that you believe could be improved through some of the techniques discussed in this chapter, tell how you would improve them.

Chapter 27

Image Advertising on Radio

While all advertising builds an image of the product or the company behind it, the term is generally used in reference to corporate advertising—in which the objective of the advertising is to create in many minds a concept of and a favorable attitude towards a corporation. The corporation can be a major company doing business nationally or it can be a local department store or chain of stores. The objective may be (on the part of the national company) to give potential customers confidence in the products it makes; to induce investment in its stock; it may be to win support for its management's attitude in a controversial issue; or it may be to establish a belief on the part of potential customers of a local department store in its reliability or the quality of merchandise it sells. Actually, image advertising treats a company as if it were a product, and its purpose is to create a preference among consumers for doing business with it instead of with competing companies or stores.

Radio is seldom assumed to be a suitable medium for image advertising. Those who make this assumption make it for a number of reasons, but largely because radio listeners are unlikely to be interested in a narration of how a business operates or what its management's beliefs are or even to believe that what they hear is other than "just advertising." But audience interest is stimulated less by what is said than by how it is said. And it should never be forgotten that one of the earliest interests a child develops is in hearing stories. This interest does not lessen as the child reaches adulthood. The very media that carry advertising—as well as countless media that do not, such as books—are physical evidence of the unceasing urge among human beings to be "told a story."

But it must *be* a story. It must begin with a situation that requires a solution and excites curiosity about what that solution may be. If there is no situation to involve the reader's or listener's interest or curiosity there is no story and no reason why the reader or listener should be eager to learn anything further. Writers of corporate advertising — especially if it is to be aired on radio — should have training in story development, in "storytelling." No skill in the writing of advertising — any kind of advertising, corporate or product — is more vital than this. Without it, an advertising message repels rather than holds its audience.

Storytelling is the one form of communication that does not require the exercise of sight. It is the one form in which words are dominant and is, therefore, vital to radio advertising. The advertiser — or the copywriter — who assumes that a radio commercial requires only the relation of product advantages has little conception of the importance of reader involvement.

In the early days of radio, the writer, Alexander Woolcott, held listeners spellbound for 30 minutes simply by telling a story. The popularity of talk shows on radio is in the issues raised and what is finally decided about them. News items are necessarily largely about fires, and murders, because there is little to arouse interest in a Boy Scout helping an old lady across a street. Sports are eagerly listened to on radio because whether they are football, baseball, basketball, boxing, or tennis, there is an unquenchable desire to learn "how they come out." Business as a function holds little of interest for most people. Yet, as those involved in it are aware, it is a human activity which, because of its highly competitive nature, has within it the absorbing element of conflict — which is precisely the factor that arouses the intense absorption of old as well as young in sports. But there are fewer writers who can write interestingly about business than there are who can write interestingly about sports. What is required is as thorough an acquaintance with business as with sports. Radio is a waiting medium on which the story of business can be told, and told skillfully. While radio is accepted as the ideal medium for reaching young people, corporate management seldom is aware of the value of arousing the interest of youth in business — despite the fact that it is from the youth market that tomorrow's business management must inevitably come. And the more it knows about the contribution of capable management to the economy in general and its own well-being and prosperity in particular, the more productive a market it can become.

QUESTIONS, SUBJECTS FOR DISCUSSION

1. Why is radio considered an unsuitable medium for corporate or "image building" advertising?

2. What is the most effective way to stimulate interest in a corporate commercial?

3. Does the lack of the opportunity to use visual treatment in a corporate advertising message provide sufficient reason for not transmitting corporate messages over it? If not, why not?

4. Why do news programs, talk programs and sports broadcasts evoke more listener interest than a totally musical program?

5. If a corporate message requires longer treatment than the standard 30-second or 60-second commercial makes possible, how can this be overcome?

6. What does the novel have in common with radio insofar as visual treatment is concerned?

PROJECT

Outline a campaign using radio to build a favorable image for a corporation, for a local department store, or for a food chain and accompany it with at least one example of how one or more of the commercials to be used in the campaign might be handled.

Chapter 28

The Jingle

Because radio is largely a musical medium, the jingle or singing commercial is and has been a most effective form of commercial message. However, it has been particularly effective on radio because a jingle is essentially a song—lyrics set to music—and can be entertaining as well as informative and memorable.

The major problem in creating a singing commercial is in successfully combining the art form—the lyrics and music—and the commercial message. It is in the jingle, in fact, more than in any other form of advertising that an advertiser can most clearly discern the importance of competent artistic talent in adding to the effectiveness of a commercial message. The creator of the jingle, however, does not always recognize the importance of having the jingle's commercial message clear and persuasive. Too often, reason is sacrificed for rhyme, and clarity and proper emphasis sacrificed for musical rhythm.

Few copywriters are adept at verse and fewer still are adept at musical composition. As a consequence, most jingles come into being at "jingle houses." No songwriter, however, can possibly be as close to and as familiar with the advertising strategy behind a product as the copywriter—who knows better than any professional lyricist what can most effectively be said about a product and exactly how it should be said to attain a maximum degree of persuasion. The copywriter, therefore, should attempt to develop at least a modicum of skill at versifying as to have some conception of how to inject skillfully the basic facts about a product into a lyric.

If a copywriter has no facility at versifying, he or she should at least list for the jingle house the principal features, advantages, and benefits of the product and the order in which they should be presented. If possible, the copywriter should attempt a lyric, no matter how unprofessional or inartistic it might be. For this purpose a rhyming dictionary is helpful in that it can save the time that would otherwise be spent finding appropriate words that rhyme with final syllables. Most rhyming dictionaries contain a thorough review of the kinds and names of verse rhythms — although these do not always lend themselves to musical rhythm. Perhaps the most infectious verse rhythm is the rhythm of the limerick and, for starters, it is not a waste of time for copywriters to familiarize themselves with the limerick and to attempt to write the lyrics for a jingle in limerick form.

Once the copywriter has become familiar with the art and technique of versifying, it is then time to try writing lines that not only contain facts about a product but conform to the rhythms of a familiar musical tune. Through these attempts, he or she may ultimately gain sufficient skill to work with a composer in writing jingles. Because of this experience in the writing of advertising, the lyrics the copywriter writes should be more effective commercially than those of someone more skilled in the writing of lyrics or of music but a stranger to advertising. Like the hit song in a musical comedy, a good jingle should be memorable, and "whistle-able." When this occurs, the message remains in the forefront of the mind of those who have heard the jingle, a mnemonic tenacity few spoken commercials have.

For this reason, jingles are especially effective for the advertising of parity products, products that have few if any advantages that competitive products do not also have. Jingles can keep the awareness of such products — as few spoken commercials can — in the listener's memory. And, of course, ultimately the principal contribution advertising of any kind makes to a product is to cause it to become familiar, recognizable, and remembered.

To be remembered, the music should not only be melodic, it should, if possible, be related to the product. For example, the Ogilvy agency created a musical theme for Maxwell House coffee that resembled the bubbly perking sound of coffee being brewed. Another example — the first detergent cleanser ever introduced came from the manufacturer of X-ray development fluid. The detergent was called Scoop — because its non-soapy nature and superior cleaning properties made it news. At the time newsboys still existed and, when they sold their papers on the street corners, they yelled, "Extra! Extra! Read all about it!" The copywriter—whose client was the X-ray Development fluid manufacturer—suddenly realized that the newsboy's cry was actually a melody:

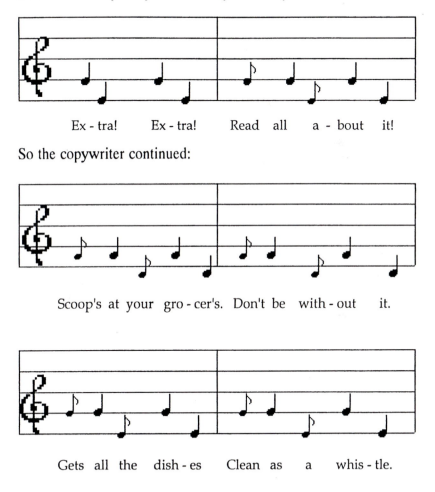

Ex - tra!   Ex - tra!   Read   all   a - bout   it!

So the copywriter continued:

Scoop's at your gro - cer's. Don't be with - out   it.

Gets   all   the   dish - es   Clean   as   a   whis - tle.

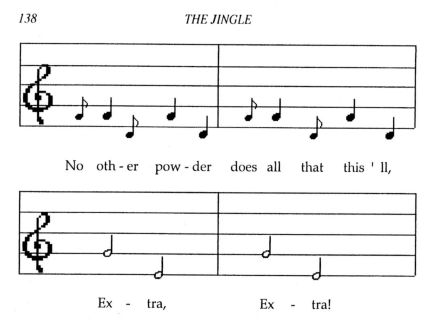

No oth - er   pow - der   does all   that   this ' ll,

Ex - tra,   Ex - tra!

The announcer then explained, with no musical background, how Scoop Detergent differed from soap and cleansed more thoroughly and that it was the only cleanser of its type available and that, despite its superior cleaning power, cost no more than soap powders. Then the jingle was resumed and closed the commercial in exactly sixty seconds.

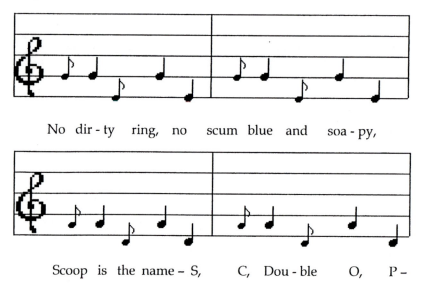

No dir - ty   ring,   no   scum blue and   soa - py,

Scoop is the name – S,   C, Dou - ble   O,   P –

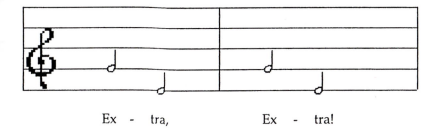

Ex - tra,   Ex - tra!

A jingle or singing commercial must say something about the product and what it will do. At the same time, the advertising claim must be integrated with the lyrics in such a way that is not only easy to sing, but is clear and understandable. Here are lyrics written for chlorophyll tablets called Stoppers. Despite the rhythm and rhyme, the lyrics are as normal as conversation:

> Don't be without Stoppers
> And you won't be without friends.
> At work, play, or at pleasure
> Unpleasant breath offends.
> To stop it nothing fills the bill
> Like Stoppers' special chlorophyll.
> So don't be without Stoppers
> And you won't be without friends.

The *Philadelphia Bulletin* at one time had a slogan, "In Philadelphia nearly everybody reads the *Bulletin*." A singing commercial featuring it might have been:

In Philadelphia nearly everybody reads the *Bulletin*.
They start with it on Monday and read it right through Sunday.

To learn what gives where each one lives
He really needs the *Bulletin* —
For all the news that's popping, for help when going shopping.

In Kensington, in Tinicum, in Cobbs Creek, and in Logan,
From Mayfair out to Sixty-ninth, events bear out this slogan —

In Philadelphia nearly everybody reads the *Bulletin*,
And if you're smart we're sure you'll start to read it, too!

QUESTIONS, SUBJECTS FOR DISCUSSION

1. Why is the jingle an effective method of doing a commercial on radio?

2. What is one of the problems in writing a commercial in lyric form?

3. In what way can a copywriter help a jingle house create a singing commercial that is as effective as a spoken commercial?

4. To what can a copywriter turn to help overcome his or her ineptness at writing a commercial in lyric form?

5. Why are jingles particularly suited to advertising a parity product?

PROJECT

Select a parity product and write a jingle advertising it.

Chapter 29

Trade Characters

One of the early forms of advertising was the inn or tavern sign, consisting generally of a name and a symbol exemplifying the name — like the White Horse Tavern with a likeness of a white horse or the Bird in Hand with a drawing of a bird held in a hand. The symbol was employed chiefly because of a general lack of literacy. At the same time, the illiterate, seeing and recognizing the symbol, could refer to it verbally. When applied to packages the symbol became known as a trademark and could be registered so that competitors could not use or exploit it. One of the best known of these was the Smith Brothers likenesses which adorned the boxes containing the cough drops of that name. A trademark had to be used strictly as it was registered if it was to remain the property of the owner. If it were altered in any way, it lost its exclusivity.

Perhaps because of this, the "trade character" came into being — the Jolly Green Giant, Speedy Alka Seltzer, the Pillsbury Doughboy and many others, all of which could be animated without danger of becoming "generic." Interesting enough, by being animated the trade character became so thoroughly associated with the product it identified that no competitor could exploit it without benefitting the owner. The Campbell Kids are a good example of this. No other canned product could use the Campbell Kids — even without the verses — without providing Campbell with advertising it did not have to pay for.

Trade characters came not only to be identified with particular products but created for the product associated with them a kind of "affection." It is not unlike the affection children develop for fairy tale characters — Goldilocks of the Three Bears; the Three Bears themselves; Jack of Jack and the Beanstalk; the Old Lady who lived in a shoe; little Jack Horner who sat in a corner. And to these the many Disney characters must be added, Mickey Mouse especially but, Minnie Mouse, Donald Duck, and Pluto as well. Despite the commercial nature of trade characters, many enjoy the empathy and the attachment the fairy tale and Disney characters enjoy.

While these characters are primarily visual, they lend themselves exceptionally well to the purely auditory medium of radio—perhaps because they are so readily visualized. It is necessary, of course, that they be mentioned when used and given verbal identity—the deep voice and Ho-ho-ho of the Jolly Green Giant, for example. Having them speak in support of the product associated with them tends to give whatever is said of the product added interest and considerably more emotional impact than could possibly be conveyed by a faceless, unidentifiable radio announcer.

To no small extent, trade characters provide the same involvement and emotional attachment that comic strip characters provide. There is by adults as well as by children an identification with and fondness for these characters that cause them to live longer and more fondly in the memory than most fictional characters in novels, plays, or motion pictures ever attain. It is to be doubted that any actual human being, even if a popular and acclaimed sports figure, could have popularized spinach as broadly as the cartoon character, Popeye. While the tendency of human beings to feel a genuine closeness and affection for these imaginary creatures is inexplicable, it is there, it is undeniable, it exists and, because it does, trade characters provide invaluable ambassadors of goodwill for the companies fortunate enough to have acquired them.

Trade characters and jingles are a "natural" combination—for radio as well as TV. The jingle is as far from normal human communication as can be imagined. As was mentioned earlier, if a real door-to-door sales representative appeared at your door and sang to you whatever he or she wished to tell you about a product—Alka Seltzer, for example—your immediate reaction would be embarrassment and possibly even fear about the level of his or her sanity. But when Speedy Alka Seltzer sang the plop-plop, fizz-fizz jingle there was an immediate acceptance and even belief in what Speedy conveyed about the product.

As a consequence, the use of trade characters in radio commercials should not be overlooked as an effective and memorable way to establish brand familiarity and acceptance. Established and well-known trade characters can speak the commercial, identifying themselves, of course, and speaking in a voice associated with their particular nature; or they can sing the commercial. Brand identification will be high and the commercial will have greater interest and longer retention than it might have in any other way. The imagination will be aroused and a visual impression will come about that most radio commercials do not produce.

QUESTIONS, SUBJECTS FOR DISCUSSION

1. What is the probable derivation of trade characters?

2. In what way do they differ from trademarks?

3. What is a likely explanation of the "affection" people come to feel about trade characters?

4. What is the advantage of this so far as the product is concerned?

5. What is an effective way to bring trade characters "alive" on radio? Give some examples.

6. On what form of radio commercial can trade characters be effectively used? Why?

PROJECT

Create a commercial involving a popular trade character in such a way that the trade character could be identified even by someone who has never seen a likeness of that character.

Chapter 30

Corporate Advertising — Radio

Radio is seldom considered as a medium for corporate advertising. Broadcast media in general — radio *and* television — are generally passed over and print media preferred. One reason, of course, is the greater diversity of print media, particularly national and even local magazines. In the print media more attention is given to business and business news. In the broadcast media the mood of the audience, which turns to both radio and television largely for entertainment, is not likely to be compatible with a corporate message which is, almost always, serious in nature. Moreover, a sizable percentage of the broadcast audience is youthful, particularly in radio. At the same time, no small part of radio's youthful audience is of college age and at college where, currently at least, the more popular courses are courses in business subjects. As a result, radio should probably be given more attention than it is for corporate advertising. In fact, it might even be considered as a recruitment medium. As for television, no small part of the audience is elderly and retired, living on income from investments and therefore quite likely to listen to corporate messages intently. It also represents a substantial voting block.

A major problem and, at the same time, a major opportunity in the creation of corporate messages for radio is the necessity of making them lively and interesting enough to hold the attention of a listening audience. It demands of whoever is writing the message greater attention to clarity in what is written and to the use in the message of language and terms that capture and maintain audience interest.

Radio's audience as well provides a good number of employed people that is almost tantamount to a captive audience during drive time, both morning and late afternoon. Whatever the aim of the corporate advertising employed, it should be treated as a thoughtful analysis, almost as news, and even as a challenging and controversial point of view. Politicians make extensive use of radio – because of both its low cost and its reach – and business can find it useful and practicable for the same reasons.

In relation to its use as a recruitment medium, it is entirely possible that management could disseminate messages over radio counselling the young in the selection of careers, not just acquainting them with where the best opportunities can be found, but the kind of training that will enable them to make the most of their careers. Business could in its own interests champion greater interest in and better command of language and mathematics than are currently found and yet are so urgently needed for American business to be effectively competitive both domestically and internationally. The use of radio in this way by business could come close to being public service as well as corporate advertising. The use of radio in recruitment applies to local businesses as well as to national corporations. If anything, it is possible this method could prove even more productive locally than nationally. Local chains or stores using radio recruitment messages could increase patronage because of parents grateful for its beneficial influence on their children. Such advertising, in addition to promoting greater interest in education, could also be employed – and this *would* be public service – to affect and improve attitudes and behavior of the young, particularly in relation to the use of tobacco, alcohol and drugs.

In addition to building goodwill, radio can be effectively used in building store image, in creating a particular concept of a store, in positioning it in order to attract a particular kind and type of customer. As pointed out in the chapter on the use of newspaper advertising for building store image, this kind of advertising can build the kind of store traffic that marketing strategy indicates will prove of greatest value to the company's present and future.

Radio offers still another advantage as a corporate medium. It has proved itself the most universal form of communication because of the immediacy of its message and because more people are able to hear and understand what is said than are able to read and comprehend what is written. This applies particularly to the growing number of Hispanics in the society who are rapidly becoming the country's major minority. Immigrants from Mexico, Puerto Rico, Cuba, the countries of Central and of South America together with no small number of people from the Far East — Vietnam, Cambodia — will be able to speak English before they can read it and radio, as a consequence, is the most effective and lowest cost means of advertising to them.

These people also need helpful information in adapting to our country and its ways. They will one day vote and not all come from countries in which democracy is the established form of government. If we are to remain a society of free enterprise, corporate advertising of an educational nature addressed to the newly arrived can prove a sound investment on the part of national corporations as well as of local businesses. And radio is beyond doubt the most certain way of reaching these people and having them comprehend what is said.

QUESTIONS, SUBJECTS FOR DISCUSSION

1. Why is radio seldom considered as an appropriate medium for corporate advertising?

2. In what particular ways, and for reaching what particular audience, can it prove especially effective?

3. What particular kind of message from business is suggested because of the large percentage of the youthful market radio reaches?

4. In what special way could radio be used to win the goodwill of parents toward either a national corporation or a local store or chain of stores?

5. What is happening to our population that makes the use of radio by business almost mandatory?

6. Why is corporate advertising on radio addressed to those who cannot yet read English easily of special importance?

PROJECT

Write a 60-second radio commercial intended to win the goodwill of young people toward a company you choose and explain why you think it will do this.

Chapter 31

Television

Unlike radio, which is addressed to hearing, and newspapers, magazines and outdoor posting, which are addressed to sight, television is addressed to both hearing and sight — and, to the sense of sight, it is addressed in motion. As a consequence, exactly as in the theater or in motion pictures, television is more readily accepted as being real, actual, lifelike. Because when what is shown on the tube is not realistic or lifelike, it is more glaringly unrealistic than might be considered in any other medium.

It is because of this that advertising on television is more criticized than advertising in or on any other medium. In fact, the most frequently made criticisms of television commercials are that they are "unreal," "phony," or "ridiculous." Viewers state emphatically that "people don't act that way in real life." This imposes an inescapable responsibility on the writer of television commercials — he or she must do more in the commercial than convey the advantages of the product; he or she must convey those advantages in a way that the viewer finds and considers a genuine imitation of life.

The criticism that a television commercial is "unreal" or "phony" or "ridiculous" is made chiefly of commercials involving dialogue and interactions between two or among three or more individuals. When the dialogue or the interaction is considered by viewers as "not being the way people act in real life," they are finding fault not with *what* is said so much as they are finding fault with *how* what is said or portrayed. It is similar to the embarrassment an audience feels watching a play written and enacted by amateurs, an embarrassment which, after too many such experiences, hardens into resentment and becomes, as in the most common summing up of television commercials, "an insult to my intelligence."

This imposes on the writer of television commercials the need to acquire such skills as are required in the writing of short stories, novels, and particularly of plays—the writing of believable dialogue, the quick development of character. Viewers watch television not to see commercials but to be entertained or amused exactly as in the theater or in the movies. If a copywriter elects to employ the stuff of storytelling or theater to convey a commercial message he or she must know or learn how to employ it. The writer, in short, must be more than a writer of advertising copy. He or she must know the basic elements of drama, comedy, and fantasy. The writer cannot afford—if he or she is to serve the client properly—to write amateurishly. The copywriter has sufficient training to know poorly written advertising copy—he or she must be equally able to recognize poorly written theater as well. A copywriter, unless trained in musical composition, will not attempt to compose the music for a singing commercial—or the lyrics for one unless skilled in versification; he or she should be as disinclined to write dialogue for a dramatized TV commercial without some knowledge or awareness of how it should be written to sound "real." As stated, television is a medium more closely related to theater than any other and must be handled exactly as theater is handled. Advertisers who use television insist on programs with high ratings and programs obtain high ratings in the same way that Broadway shows attain S.R.O. signs at the box office. Advertisers should demand of the commercials they are asked to accept for showing on, or adjacent to, such programs the same audience-pleasing qualities.

There is no reason whatsoever that a persuasive message cannot be made interesting, even entertaining. It has been done many times—and yet all too few times, considering the plethora of television commercials inflicted on the viewing public daily. There are erroneous beliefs among advertisers and many agency people that commercials that win awards win those awards at the expense of their practical reason for being—to induce viewers to purchase or make use of the product or service featured. There is ample evidence to disprove this. When the high cost of television time compelled advertisers to use 30-second commercials instead of 60-second commercials, the opportunity to create interest and entertainment was considerably reduced. Yet the 30-second commercials for the Polaroid Instant Camera done by James Garner and Mariette Hartley were of sufficient interest to create a movie career for Ms. Hartley. It is of interest to note that the writer of those commercials, Jack Dillon, also wrote five novels and more than a hundred short stories.

The viewing public, by and large, objects to having the programs it watches interrupted by commercials. Little can be done about this, but much could be done to make the commercials, whenever they appear, entertaining to watch. The "Mikey" commercial for Life cereal, for example, was on the air for thirteen years and, despite its obvious familiarity was constantly enjoyed by viewers — many of whom when the commercial, because of its age, was removed, wrote the advertiser asking what had happened to Mikey. A commercial for Coca Cola featuring Mean Joe Green actually elicited praise from viewers. It is evident, therefore, that commercials can be created that viewers find as acceptable and entertaining as the programs they interrupt. Even commercials lacking in story situations, commercials devoted totally to a description of the product and its advantages, can be made enjoyable. The James Garner-Mariette Hartley commercials for Polaroid already referred to, are a notable example.

What is said and what is shown in a television commercial are important, but *how* it is said and *how* it is shown are of equal if not greater importance. As for what is said, it should be well said, it should be clear, it should avoid — just like print advertising — the typical advertising cliches. It should be said in language and in a tone of voice that conveys a determination to be helpful to the viewer, not simply to "sell" something. What is shown should avoid the visual cliches common to all too many television commercials. The so-called "slice of life" commercials, for example, were so overdone they became no longer a slice of "life." As the old saying has it, no matter how thin you slice it, it is still baloney. Remember that television is theater and whether a real life situation is shown or the commercial is humorous or is done as a fantasy, it must be done in such a way that the viewer likes it, accepts it, does not find it false or contrived or annoying. Remember the commercials that you find false or annoying and avoid those elements in the commercials you do.

The so-called "stand-up" commercial—the announcer simply standing before the camera and delivering the commercial—is generally spoken at the rate of two words a second. The current widely used 15-second commercial—if of the stand-up variety—allows a commercial length of only thirty words. As a consequence, while it can contain the mention of a product benefit, it is too short to be as persuasive as a 30- or 60-second commercial. It should be treated, therefore, as an ID or 10-second spot shown between programs—an idea covered in Chapter 38.

HOW TO SET UP A TYPEWRITTEN TV COMMERCIAL

Fundamental Instructions

1. Assume the page on which you are typing your TV commercial to be divided in half. Over the middle of left side type the word VIDEO and over the middle of right side type the word AUDIO.

2. All video descriptions and instructions should be in CAPS.

3. Every scene should be preceded with an indication whether it is to be a long shot (LS), or a medium long shot (MLS), a medium shot (MS), a close-up (CU) or an extreme close-up (ECU).

4. If camera is to move slowly across scene, instruction is PAN. If a scene is to fade out, write FADE OUT. If it is to dissolve into a following scene, write DISSOLVE.

5. Include in video section any print message, indicated SUPER.

6. In audio section, all conversation is to be typed in caps and lower case because lower case is easier to read than caps.

7. Coordinate audio sections with video sections by numbers.

8. Characters' names in audio section and any instructions (such as sound effects—SFX) are to be in caps.

9. Remember that everything that is *seen* is to be described under VIDEO and everything that is to be *heard* is to be described under AUDIO.

10. If anything happens *later* in a scene such as the arrival of another character, but the scene itself does not change, number it 1A or 2A or 3A, etc.

Example

Wellington
TV — 60 seconds

1. DARK SCREEN.	1. WIFE: Darling. Someone's in our bedroom.
2. LIGHTS GO ON. MLS OF BURGLARS, – TWO OF THEM – ONE WITH REVOLVER, THE OTHER HOLDING DIAMONDS, INCLUDING NECKLACE.	2. BURGLAR WITH DIAMONDS: Stay where you are. All we want's these rocks.
3. CU OF WOMAN IN BED, HOLDING COVERS UP TO HERSELF.	3. WOMAN: But they're not real. They're counterfeit.
4. SAME AS 2.	4. BURGLAR WITH DIAMONDS: Lady, I know real rocks when I see 'em.
5. CU OF HUSBAND.	5. HUSBAND: I'll make you a deal. BURGLAR (V.O.): Yeah? HUSBAND: If you can get a hundred thousand for them, keep them. If you can't, bring them back. Okay?
6. BURGLARS BACK TOWARD OPEN WINDOWS.	6. BURGLAR: Okay. It's a deal.
7. DISSOLVE TO MLS OF HUSBAND AND WIFE ON DIVAN IN LIVING ROOM. IT IS THE NEXT DAY.	7. HUSBAND: Some experience we had last night. SFX: SOUND OF WINDOW BREAKING.

8. MCU OF FLOOR. SMALL PACKAGE LANDS ON IT.	8. WIFE: What's that?
9. MCU OF HUSBAND ON HANDS AND KNEES ON FLOOR. HE PICKS UP PACKAGE.	9. HUSBAND: It's the Wellington Counterfeit Diamonds. And a note that says, "Like you said, it's a deal. Here are your phony rocks. And I thought we knew the real thing when we saw it."
10. CU OF TWO DIAMONDS ON A PIECE OF BLACK VELVET. POINTER POINTS TO FIRST DIAMOND, THEN TO SECOND.	10. ANNOUNCER (V.O.): Cost of genuine white diamond—fifteen thousand dollars a carat. Cost of a look-the-same Wellington Counterfeit Diamond—one hundred and thirty-five dollars a carat. And it looks for real.
11. BLACK SCREEN. ON R. IS CARICATURE OF MADAME WELLINGTON. ON LEFT IS SUPER: CALL TOLL FREE 800 000-0000.	

QUESTIONS, SUBJECTS FOR DISCUSSION

1. Because television, of all media of communication, comes closest to presenting life and living as it appears to be, why is it difficult to write believable commercials to appear on it?

2. What does television make essential in writing commercials to appear on it that other media do not require to the same degree?

3. Why is it that, of all forms of advertising, people are more critical of TV commercials?

4. What skills should a copywriter develop in order to write television commercials that do not "insult the intelligence" of viewers?

5. Why is it not sufficient simply to be able to relate in a televi-

sion commercial the advantages and benefits of the product or service advertised?

6. What problems does a 30-second as opposed to a 60-second TV commercial present to a copywriter?

PROJECT

Do a 60-second TV commercial about a product or a service in dramatized form; then do a 30-second version of it.

Chapter 32

The Stand-Up Pitch

The simplest and least expensive television commercial is the so-called "stand-up pitch" — or a commercial delivered by a single individual. While it is one of the most difficult commercial forms to make interesting, it can be, depending on the personality of the "pitch man," one of the most convincing forms of product presentation, perhaps because of its one-to-one nature or one individual talking to another.

As stated, a stand-up commercial can be delivered understandably at the rate of two words a second. Some announcers can speak at a faster rate and still be understood. However, the more words employed, the faster it must be spoken, and the more difficult it is to understand.

The background in the stand-up pitch commercial can vary widely. The commercial can be delivered in so-called limbo — against a plain background — or, if the product is an automobile, it can be delivered by the announcer seated before the steering wheel of the car — even presumably driving it, with a filmed background providing the illusion of motion. What is said would appear to be more important than what is seen. Many stand-up pitch commercials are delivered in limbo with the announcer holding the product, pointing at it, or advancing it towards the camera — with the label, of course, facing the lens. This method of focusing attention on the product has been used so many times that it has become a visual cliche and should be avoided.

Charts and other visual aids are occasionally employed to intensify and make the claim or claims made for the product more memorable — such as greater strength for an analgesic. By and large, the stand-up pitch has little drama unless it is delivered by a well-known personality whose appearance and voice add interest. A stand-up pitch delivered, for example, by Marcel Marceau, the famous mime, could be absorbing and the message, performed instead of spoken, could be memorable to an exceptional degree.

In the stand-up pitch commercial, as in any kind of television commercial, every effort should be made to avoid the usual, the expected. In attempting the unusual, however, whatever is done should not be of such a nature as to dilute the sincerity of what is said — like having an opera star sing the commercial in operatic fashion and, in doing so, reduce it to absurdity. If a demonstration were involved, however, say of a high fidelity tape, an opera star could be used quite effectively to sing the commercial standing before a curtain. Then, after the star stopped singing, the voice continued and the curtain was pulled back to reveal its source: a tape on playback.

A commercial delivered by a well-known comedian, in character, could have an exceptional interest factor — but the product would have to be one that lent itself to being described humorously — a candy bar, a collapsible umbrella, certainly not a fine piece of furniture, or even a food product. The nature of the comedian and the particular kind of comedy are factors that must be considered. Bill Cosby, for example, has appeared in commercials, was amusing, and in no way failed to establish interest and confidence in the product.

As stated previously, television is "show business." News itself, for example, does not and cannot vary from station to station. But news *programs* vary in interest and ratings in direct relation to the personalities who deliver the news — their appearance, their voice, and their particular style of delivery. Studies have shown that audiences have greater confidence in the accuracy of news as given by certain personalities. No less do commercials compete for interest, acceptance and belief; and the copywriter who knows something of the techniques of theatrical presentation has an advantage over the copywriter who lacks this knowledge in the production of interest-evoking, sales-inducing, non-irritating commercials.

QUESTIONS, SUBJECTS FOR DISCUSSION

1. Why is the so-called "stand-up pitch" commercial a difficult type of commercial to write?

2. Why at the same time does the "stand-up pitch" occasionally prove more persuasive, and convincing than a dramatized commercial?

3. In what ways can audience interest in a "stand-up pitch" commercial be heightened?

4. What are some of the problems of using well-known comedians in "stand-up pitch" commercials?

5. What is a very clear example of the show-business nature of television?

6. What can be derived from an awareness of this insofar as the writing of television commercials is concerned?

PROJECT

Do a "stand-up pitch" commercial for a product of your choice using a personality, if you wish, and doing the commercial either in limbo or against a particular background.

Chapter 33

Demonstration

Demonstration and sampling—two words, actually, for the same process: trying the product—are generally regarded as the most effective ways to sell anything. Sampling is not possible on television but demonstration is, and one of the prime strengths of television as an advertising medium is that, on it, demonstration of a product can be as close to having the actual product demonstrated before you as is possible. You can watch as a photograph comes into being on instant film. You can hear a "beeper" notifying a doctor to call the office. You can see how a typing mistake on a typewriter with delayed printing is corrected before it appears on the page being typed. There is no need to "stop at your local dealer" to determine what a product looks like or how it functions. If you "stop at your local dealer" it will most likely be to purchase rather than inspect the product.

It can be argued that, in print, these same products can be demonstrated through a series of still photographs. And it is true. The emerging picture on instant film can be shown in stages of its appearance. How mistakes are corrected on a delayed printing typewriter before they are printed can also be shown. Successive photographs can show a doctor presumably hearing the beeper and going to a nearby telephone booth. But these lack the actuality of continuous action and sound. In a print ad, bold type can claim an acceleration potential of 0 mph to 60 mph in ten seconds for a car—and the reader, believing in the integrity of the medium as well as of the advertiser, will accept it as fact. But it can never carry the conviction of a commercial showing on a split screen, a speedometer, to left, rising from 0 miles an hour to 60 while, on the right, a stopwatch ticks off the seconds and, in the background, the roar of the motor is evident.

The manner in which a demonstration is conducted is vital to the degree of conviction obtained by it. Viewers *expect* the advertised product not to fail knowing that, if it did, the commercial would not be shown. The demonstration must be one in which the process employed to prove product efficacy is complete. Consider a Tums commercial in which two phials of what is said to be stomach acid are shown. In one a Tums tablet is stirred; in the other, a Rolaids tablet. In each bottle, the slightly opaque liquid becomes crystal clear. To prove the greater strength of Tums over Rolaids, additional stomach acid is poured into each phial. The phial in which the Rolaids tablet has been dropped becomes slightly opaque again while the liquid into which the Tums tablet was stirred remains clear. The relation of the amount of acid in each phial to the amount of acid in a stomach that needs alkalinizing is never stated. It could be assumed by the viewer—who is suspicious anyway—that the amounts used were determined by what was needed to cause the Tums tablet to appear as if it were more effective in settling stomach discomfort.

By contrast, consider a commercial developed to show the clarity and reality of a particular brand of television set. The opening shot is a close-up of a canary. A cat is shown approaching the canary and finally pouncing on it. The camera draws back to show the cat pouncing on the tube of a TV set showing the canary. There is no doubt that the portrayal of the canary was clear and realistic enough to have caused the cat to assume the canary was real.

The potential of realistic portrayal that television offers demands of those who write commercials for it the utmost in skill and sensitivity to achieve realism. When it is not achieved, when it is done in such a way that the viewer finds it lacking in realism, the failure is as impactful in destroying acceptance of the product as convincing realism would have been in achieving it—which is why the writer must be as critical as the viewer will be. The advertiser is at a disadvantage in determining how convincing the demonstration is because he or she is so determined to prove the superiority of the product and so overwhelmingly certain of that superiority that it is almost impossible for him or her to see the commercial as the viewer will see it. The writer is at a similar disadvantage if he or she considers the demonstration itself more important than the manner in which it is conducted. In short, television — more than any other medium — is ideal for the most effective kind of selling: demonstration. But because it is, in addition, the most theatrical of media, commercials done for it must be done with the highest sensitivity and with a realization that the public is basically skeptical of any attempt to sell something.

In terms of demonstration, it is ironic to consider that no matter how much effort is put into a commercial to show the enjoyment of a food or a beverage, to demonstrate its desirability, conviction is seldom achieved. The person sipping the beverage or biting the food can sip or bite and look pleased and exclaim, "mmmm!" or "ahhh!" without in any way conveying delight convincingly to the viewer.

Following are two examples of how to attain believable dialogue in a commercial. The first can be accepted as the way two boys might discuss running away from home. The second — because it is a humorous sketch — provides the necessary "suspension of disbelief" intense or humorous drama brings about.

Campbell Soup Company
Chunky Soups
TV spot — 60 second

VIDEO	AUDIO
1. LS OF BOY 1 WALKING DOWN COUNTRY LANE. HE IS WEARING STRAW HAT. IN HIS LEFT HAND HE IS CARRYING A CRUDE FISHING POLE.	1. BOY 2: Whatcha doin'? BOY 1: Runnin' away from home. BOY 2: Where you gonna live? BOY 1: Down by the crick. BOY 2: Whatcha gonna eat? BOY 1: Fish.

IN HIS RIGHT HAND
HE HOLDS A STICK
OVER HIS SHOULDER
WITH A CLOTH BAG
SWINGING FROM IT.
BOY 2 RUNS IN FROM
CAMERA R AND JOINS
BOY 1. CAMERA PRECEDES
THEM AS THEY WALK
DOWN ROAD.

BOY 2: Supposin' ya don't ketch
any?
BOY 1: I gotta can of Campbell's
Chunky Soup.
BOY 2: You're gonna need more
than soup.
BOY 1: Mom says Campbell's
Chunky *is* more than soup. It's got
big chunksa meat and stuff.
BOY 2: Supposin' ya get tired
of it?
BOY 1: I got crackers, too.

1A. BOY 2 STOPS. SO DOES
    BOY 1.

BOY 2: I got an idea. Why doncha
wait'll after lunch and I'll run
away *with* ya?
BOY 1: Okay. But you gotta bring
your own Chunky Soup.

2. CU. CAMERA PANS PAST
    ROW OF CHUNKY SOUPS.

ANNOUNCER (V.O.)
Campbell's Chunky Soup. Large
chunks of everything, as in soup
you make yourself. And you don't
have to leave home to enjoy it.

General Foods
International Coffees
TV spot—30 seconds

VIDEO	AUDIO
1. MS TWO MECHANICS ON FLOOR OF KITCHEN REPAIRING DISHWASHER.	1. MIKE: My troat's dry as a unused spare tiah. PETE: Mine, too.
2. CU OF MIKE.	2. MIKE: Miz Jones? You got maybe some java for two toisty guys? MRS. JONES (OFF CAMERA): I just made some!

3. MRS. JONES ENTERS WITH TRAY CONTAINING TWO CUPS OF COFFEE. MIKE AND PETE EACH TAKE ONE.	3. MRS. JONES: This is General Foods International Coffee. This is Café Français. MIKE: Imagine dat, Pete — real French coffee!
4. MCU OF MIKE AND PETE AS THEY SIP.	4. MIKE: Great stuff, hey, Pete? PETE: C'est très bon! MIKE: C'est très *bon*? C'est *magnifique!*
5. CU OF FIVE INTERNATIONAL COFFEES.	5. ANNOUNCER (V.O.): Try all five of General Foods exciting International Coffees — Irish Mocha Mist, Orange Cappucino, Swiss Mocha, Café Vienna and Café Français. MIKE: (V.O.): Ces sont *toutes* magnifique!

QUESTIONS, SUBJECTS FOR DISCUSSION

1. Why are demonstrations and sampling the most effective ways to sell anything?

2. Give some examples — apart from those given in the chapter — of demonstrations suited for presentation on TV.

3. Why are demonstrations on television more effective than they are in any other medium?

4. Because they have so effective a potential, why do they inevitably run the risk of being total failures?

5. In what ways are an advertiser and the writer of a television commercial at a disadvantage in criticizing one?

PROJECT

Do a commercial in which the enjoyment to be derived from eating of any food or candy or drinking of any beverage is convincingly demonstrated. If you cannot do such a demonstration, explain why.

Chapter 34

Dramatization vs. Dialogue

A dramatized commercial is one that has a "plot" or is told in story form. It enlists the viewer's interest by creating a situation of which he or she wants to learn the solution or "how it turns out" or simply "what happens." For example, a man is shown walking down a street carrying a brief case. He happens to glance upward and sees a church steeple with a clock in it. As he notices the clock it strikes three. He then looks at his wristwatch, stops, and enters the church. He makes his way up the winding staircase of the steeple until he reaches the clock's mechanism. He looks again at his wristwatch, then turns a small wheel in the mechanism. As he does, the exterior of the clock is shown with the main hand moving back so that the time on the clock is two minutes before three. The man then descends the steps and returns to the street—where he looks again at his wristwatch which shows the time as just three o'clock. He glances at the steeple clock as it again strikes three, whereupon he smiles with satisfaction and continues walking. By that time the viewer's interest has reached a point, that requires an explanation of why the man did what he did—which an announcer gives, voice over. The explanation is that anyone with a watch as accurate as an Accutron cannot tolerate any timepiece that is inaccurate.

This is the essence of a dramatized commercial. If two or more persons were involved—such as the man and a woman—there would have been dialogue. The woman, when the man stopped to look at his watch, might ask, "What's the matter?" He might say, "I'll be right back" and enter the church to climb the stairs to the steeple. When he returned to where the woman was waiting, she might ask, "What in the world were you doing?" and he might reply, "You'll see"—at which point the steeple clock would strike three and the man would show his wristwatch to the woman pointing to the same time on its face. The dialogue would be quite natural and might add to the interest of the commercial.

In a commercial in which two women discuss the problem one is having in finding a floor wax that leaves no residue on a baby's clothes when it crawls over linoleum, dialogue is essential but what is actually taking place in no way arouses any curiosity about what will occur. It is a commercial for which it is next to impossible to write believable dialogue. It is the typical TV commercial that most TV viewers regard as "unreal" or "phony," about which they say, "It doesn't happen that way in real life." The writer, in order to create a "real life" conversation, must write dialogue that viewers will believe is what real people would actually say. No type of commercial is more challenging for the writer who believes that, to be most effective, a television commercial must be realistic and believable.

The reason so many commercials of that genre are not realistic is due largely to the absence of a belief on the part of the writers that television commercials (or, for that matter, radio commercials) do not have to be realistic so long as they convey to viewers what the advertiser wants said about the product — and too many advertisers have no conception that advertising, if it is to be outstanding in communication, requires the same literary skill as any other form of writing. Too many advertisers believe that when advertising is written "well" it is likely to "sell" poorly and that a writer dedicated to making advertising as interesting and human as possible is more interested in "winning awards" than in selling products. It is a lamentable situation and, insofar as television advertising or any form of advertising is concerned, can be shown by countless actual examples to be totally unfounded.

People *do* discuss relative merits of products. They *do* make laudatory comments about products they find exceptional in one way or another. They *are* pleased and even delighted with products whose flavor they enjoy, whose performance they welcome, whose durability they value. But if actors portraying such people on television commercials are given dialogue to read that is not what real people would actually say, the degree of conviction in what is said about the product is necessarily and inevitably lessened.

For the past one hundred years, advertising has made a free press possible. It has made a magazine industry possible that could not exist without the revenue advertising provides. And it has made radio and television entertainment possible. In doing so, however, advertising has also made of itself a form of communication which, to be most effective, must borrow from other art forms. Those who would practice advertising with merit and profit must, as a consequence, achieve some degree of competence in other art forms. The advertiser who would extract from advertising its maximum contribution to business and the sale of products must not only understand this but insist upon it.

It is helpful to a copywriter to read aloud the commercials he or she has written for either television or radio and to listen critically to them. It can assist the writer in making the conversation in these commercials more like everyday conversation as well as illustrate word combinations that are difficult to say. Most important, however, is the assistance it gives the writer in making the conversation sound like genuine conversation and not like advertising.

QUESTIONS, SUBJECTS FOR DISCUSSION

1. What is a dramatized commercial and what is the main contribution it makes to an advertising message?

2. What is a dialogue commercial?

3. What is the primary way in which a dialogue commercial can influence television viewers to become interested in the product about which it is written?

4. What is the most plausible explanation of television viewers considering so many dramatized or dialogue commercials "unreal" or "phony?"

5. In what ways do advertisers unknowingly but certainly contribute to the production of TV commercials viewers consider an "insult" to their intelligence?

6. Do you believe that people actually speak highly of certain products and are sincerely delighted with qualities they offer?

7. What is a useful way in which to achieve believable conversation in both dramatized and dialogue commercials?

PROJECT

Write both a dramatized commercial and a dialogue commercial, in the latter of which people conversing convey to television viewers the superiority of one product over another.

Chapter 35

Testimonials

Persons, who for one reason or another, become well-known gain a charisma, an aura, that causes others to experience a wonder and an intense curiosity about them and anything associated with them. As a consequence, advertisers find that testimonials from such individuals, related to the product and used in its advertising, not only obtain greater interest in the advertising (as Starch studies verify) but greater interest in the product as well. This occurs despite the fact that individuals generally believe that celebrities say what they do about products because they have been paid to say it.

At one time it was possible for an advertiser to pay a celebrity to say what the advertiser wished him or her to say, whether the celebrity used the product or not. Today, however, celebrities can provide an advertiser with a testimonial only if they can demonstrate that they have used the product. Celebrities, of course, are still paid to say what the advertiser or advertising agent wishes them to say but only if they agree to. They can insist on saying what they would prefer to say.

Testimonials in print advertising present the writer with less of a problem than testimonials in broadcast advertising, particularly in a television commercial. In broadcast advertising, what is said by the celebrity must sound as if it were involuntary. If it sounds as if it were written to be said, the viewer — while fascinated by the appearance of the celebrity — is much more likely to find what is said "just advertising" than if he or she were to read the same words in print. The greater degree of realism in television — the actual "presence" of the celebrity — requires that the celebrity be realistic or at least in character; and the writer must be aware of this if the testimonial is to be accepted as the genuine reaction of the celebrity.

The writer can choose, if the testifier is a comedian, to write the testimonial "in character," with the comedian lightly jesting about the product or even about giving the testimonial, and still attain the end of investing the product with more interest for the viewer. And the reason is that the viewer can accept what the comedian says in jest because *he or she expects* humor from a comedian. The viewer might even feel that the comedian is demonstrating a certain "affection" for the product.

If the celebrity can recite an actual experience in using a product, interest in both the commercial and the product will be heightened since the public generally likes to hear as well as to read about the experiences of celebrities. Moreover, a commercial with such a testimonial is not unlike a TV talk show in which celebrities are interviewed and recall experiences they have had. It is the very stuff of television and, because it is, must be handled in the same fashion — believably. Repeatedly it has been maintained in these pages that advertising should bear some resemblance to the nature of the medium that carries it. It is sufficient in magazines, for example, for the advertising to be as informative as the editorial material. It is *not* sufficient in television for the advertising to consist simply of actors speaking lines against appropriate backgrounds; the acting, the lines, and what happens must be good theater as well as good advertising. And the discipline that makes for good theater is especially necessary in the writing and producing of television commercials featuring a testimonial — whether from a celebrity or from an unknown and unnamed individual.

This is just as important when an established authority is employed to endorse a product rather than simply to say he or she has enjoyed it. It is good theater, for example, to have the actor taped against a background relevant to the field in which he or she is an authority. It lends authenticity and believability.

The copywriter must remember the difference between a person who gives a testimonial about a product and a person who endorses it, who states not just that he or she has used it and enjoyed it but that it is "good" for the viewer or for a pet of the viewer or will contribute to longer life for the roof of the viewer's house. The endorsement of a product and what is claimed it will do or accomplish must be given by someone qualified by training and experience to know what is being talked about. A certain celebrity, for example, might say that he loves his dog and wants him to have only the best and as a result feeds his dog the brand of dog food being advertised which the dog seems to enjoy and thrive on. However, he cannot state what the food will do for the dog's health because of particular ingredients it contains unless his background — as a recognized breeder of dogs, for example — qualifies him to make the statement.

This becomes a problem with over the counter (O.T.C.) remedies such as analgesics, cough remedies, or any formulated product that is used for relief of any kind since physicians cannot be used in advertising. There was a time when advertisers got around this by having the individual recommending the product wear a white coat and a reflector strapped around the head. The so-called "white coat law" put an end to this. Insofar as doctor endorsement is concerned, the statement can be made and is made that a product is prescribed by more doctors than any other product of its kind or is even prescribed by "most" doctors — if, of course, research has determined that it actually is. This implies endorsement but actually it is not — it enables the public to conclude that the product must be effective or it would not be prescribed by so many physicians.

There are packages that have statements printed on them about the products that have been approved by the Food and Drug Administration which may be used in a commercial. Generally, however, these statements must be used exactly as approved and this makes any commercial containing them sound false when given. To overcome this, the announcer can hold up the package and say, "As you can read on the package," and then read the statement.

As this chapter tries to make clear, the use of celebrities and authorities in television commercials — or, for that matter, radio commercials — can be very effective and persuasive if handled in a way that is not only permissible but sounds true. It is not enough that it *is* true; it must be presented in a manner in which the viewer finds no problem in assuming it is.

QUESTIONS, SUBJECTS FOR DISCUSSION

1. What are the advantages in using a celebrity to deliver a commercial?

2. What is the major hindrance in using a celebrity in a commercial?

3. How can this best be overcome?

4. What is the difference in legal requirements between a person who gives a testimonial for a product and a person who endorses it?

5. What is the white coat law?

6. What is the closest you can come to an actual physician's endorsement of a product?

7. How can you avoid stiltedness in a commercial in which a character necessarily says about a product a statement permitted to be printed on the package about it?

PROJECT

Write a commercial giving either a testimonial about or an endorsement of a product. Keep the commercial to 30 seconds.

Chapter 36

Corporate Advertising — Television

Business, as a subject, is boring to most people. In addition, few copywriters have had management experience. As a consequence, most corporate advertising tends not only to seem dull, but is not given the interest it needs and should have to accomplish its purpose. The primary need is for more copywriters to have a thorough comprehension of business and its operation. One solution might be to find copywriters who have had management experience.

There is little doubt that business has been made not only interesting but absorbing in such novels as Cameron Hawley's *Executive Suite* or Frederic Wakeman's *The Hucksters*. But the former was interesting because of the conflicts among officers competing for the presidency of a company; and the latter by the terrifyingly dominant corporate head, Evan Llewelyn Evans. Neither of these situations lends itself to devising a corporate commercial intended to create goodwill, the general objective of a corporate campaign. Both novels make it quite clear, however, that aspects of a business can be found to make business an interesting subject.

One aspect of business that modern managements like to hold forth on is technological accomplishment. Treated simply as a technological accomplishment, technology offers little of dramatic value. Nevertheless, it is frequently possible — if the writer probes — to find something of general interest in the results of technology. For example, some years ago International Paper decided to use television to advertise its paper-making technology, its ability and capacity to manufacture paper in ways that had never before been possible. One way was to make a paper that had unbelievable wet strength yet retained the characteristics of paper that had no wet strength whatsoever. Another way was making paper that had equally unbelievable strength and durability but was still very light in weight.

The former paper process was shown on a television commercial that opened with a long shot of Ali McGraw on a sandy beach, wearing a bikini and about to enter the water. As she walked forward she explained that her bikini was made of a paper that had been developed by International Paper, and that it had such a high degree of wet strength she could swim in it – whereupon she dove into the water. The camera showed her swimming below the surface and then her face emerging. As she tread water she explained that because the bikini was made of paper and was therefore inexpensive, after you used it, if you wished, you could throw it away – at which point, she undid the bra of the bikini as she continued treading water, lifted it above the surface and threw it over the lens of the camera, closing the commercial.

To demonstrate the results of the latter process, the commercial opened with a long shot of a chasm, at the very top of which was a bridge. The next shot showed the underside of the bridge which appeared to be made of corrugated cardboard. A long shot into the valley below showed a truck on its way to the summit. At the summit the truck approached the bridge and dramatically stopped before crossing it. A close-up showed the wheel as it inched its way onto the bridge. As it did, the corrugated cardboard sank slightly under the tire as the weight of the truck was imposed on it. A long shot showed the truck crossing, reaching the other side, and proceeding at normal speed. Attention was then drawn again to the bridge as a helicopter, with lines attached to the bridge, lifted it and flew away with the bridge hanging from it. Like the McGraw shot in the bikini, this was actually a *demonstration* – for which television is better suited than any other medium. Nobody could doubt the extent of the technology that made both uses of paper possible but each was shown in a way that could not possibly bore, a way permitting management to show the extent of its technology and at the same time not only convince viewers of it but do so in a way viewers could not resist watching.

Probably, because of the difficulty of finding creative talent imaginative enough to make technological achievement or other aspects of business operation dramatic and interesting, many businesses turn to sponsoring service messages—on the totally valid assumption that the public will see in this the humanity of the corporation and its management. If public service sponsorship can be done in such a way as to *relate it to the particular activity* of the corporation, the credit given the corporation can extend beyond merely creating goodwill. For example, at one time Mobil ran an extremely dramatic commercial showing an automobile slung under a helicopter being flown to the roof of a 30-story skyscraper. The announcer, voice over, specifically stated the height of the building because, as he explained, an automobile dropped from such a height would meet the pavement below with the same impact as if it were being driven along a road at sixty miles an hour and rammed into another car. The car was then poised on the edge of the building and thrust over. The camera followed its fall until it smashed against the sidewalk. The announcer then stated that the purpose of the commercial was to show what can happen to a car driven at too high a speed and said that Mobil had done this because it wanted the viewer to remain alive. Another example of a company using a public service message to show its own concern for the environment was a DuPont commercial that showed a man and a garden he had grown over the years with strong and thriving flowers despite the nearness of a large chemical plant. The camera then lifted to show the chemical plant less than a quarter mile away. It was a DuPont chemical plant.

Because television is a strongly visual medium, a copywriter given the assignment of creating a corporate message to be used on television, once he or she has been told and understands what corporate management wishes to convey, should—either alone or in company with an art director—try to conceive of a dramatic visual interpretation of the message. The qualifying adjective "dramatic" is important to keep in mind. Texaco, for example, had a series of corporate commercials that featured Bob Hope but showed Hope in a hard hat pointing out and referring to technical equipment at a refinery. It was a waste of Hope's talent, the management's money, and the viewers' time.

The visual interpretation of corporate messages is challenging and requires a great deal of meditation on the part of the copywriter and the art director. Many times it can prove helpful for them to discuss the problem with the company selected to produce the commercial which may have had and solved a similar assignment from which an effective solution can be drawn.

For example, if the point the corporation wishes to make deals with a difference that requires verbal explanation, interest can be added by having a well-known and respected personality deliver the message – or by having two popular news commentators debate the situation (if it is a strike, for example, with one commentator giving labor's point of view and the other, management's).

The copywriter must always begin by trying to conceive the most effective way in which to arrive at an arresting and fascinating commercial for the public to watch and listen to. He or she must realize that a corporate message itself holds little interest for a television viewer who has turned on the set to be entertained. As a result, a corporate commercial requires the injection of more interest than a commercial intended to sell a product or a service. As in all advertising, the attitude of the creator towards what is written is the principal determinant of how well done and how brilliantly executed the finished piece will be. However, it applies particularly to corporate advertising.

QUESTIONS, SUBJECTS FOR DISCUSSION

1. What should be a copywriter's first thought when given a corporate message to be delivered over TV?

2. What special advantages does television offer an advertiser with a corporate message?

3. To what source can a copywriter and an art director turn for help in arriving at a dramatic way of telling a corporate story visually?

4. If there is actually no way to tell a corporate story with interest, in what way can a corporation use the television medium to build goodwill for itself?

5. In relation to the above, how can the espousing of a public service project best build respect for the corporation sponsoring it?

PROJECT

Re-do a corporate advertisement you have seen on TV or in print in a newspaper or a magazine. If the advertisement or the commercial fails to convey to you what its objective actually is, call or write the company's advertising director, explain your assignment and ask the advertising director whatever questions you must to learn the objective of the message.

Chapter 37

Products that Offend

Despite current candor in human relationships, there are certain products which viewers find objectionable — products associated with feminine hygiene, denture cleansers and adhesives, or hemorrhoid ointments, for example. There appears to be less objection to the advertising of these items in print media than on television. It is possible that because television is usually viewed by a group that embarrassment is felt. It is also possible that the manner in which these products are presented brings about viewers' unfavorable reactions. In a typical denture cleanser commercial, for example, a presumed denture wearer was asked if she believes Efferdent removes tea stains from dentures. When she said that she does, she was asked if she believes Efferdent removes tea *and* cherry stains. She expressed some doubt and was then asked if she believes Efferdent removes tea, cherry, *and* tobacco stains. Replying in the negative, she was asked to watch while darkly stained denture-shaped models were put into a beaker of water into which an Efferdent tablet was dropped with a resulting fizz. When the denture model was removed, it was stainless and the denture wearer was not only pleasantly surprised but said that she was going home "right now" to use Efferdent.

This is a situation that, like all too many such situations in television commercials, is unlikely to occur in real life. It is contrived and all too obviously bears the stamp of the advertiser. There is little need for what occurs because it is so obvious that Efferdent is in no way going to be shown to be ineffective. And it is undoubtedly the assumption that viewers will accept the staged demonstration as proof of Efferdent's capacity for removing stains while viewers quite accurately condemn it as an "insult" to their intelligence. The objection would appear to be less to advertising the product than to how it is advertised.

A commercial for a particular brand of tampons featured a popular female gymnast who confides to the audience that she prefers the brand mentioned because of its absorbency which allows her to perform without experiencing any fear or unease. She then does a handstand, spreading her legs fore and aft and exposing her crotch. The basic concept—that if a gymnast, considering the activity she engages in while performing, finds the tampons effective, they must be—is entirely plausible. The major objection was the attention given the crotch. Again, what is found lacking in taste is not the advertising of the product so much as the way in which it is advertised.

Judgment must be employed in determining how these products are to have their benefits made known, particularly visually. It is useful, in determining how best to handle the advertising of such products, to look for commercials about them. If the viewer has a VCR, he or she can tape the commercials for further analysis and study. If not, the viewer should, while watching, be equipped with a tablet and a pencil to note quickly the video as well as the audio, because each can contribute to the commercial's being considered "objectionable."

For example, when a denture adhesive is advertised on TV, the commercial usually begins with someone having difficulty retaining upper dentures. (The expression is "they slip.") The actor is then told by a friend that he or she had a similar problem until discovering the brand being advertised. An announcer at that point is usually shown at a small table on which there is a tube of the adhesive. Unscrewing the cap, the announcer squeezes a length of the adhesive onto the underside of the right forefinger. Then placing the tube on the table, the announcer presses the coated forefinger against the tube and is able to raise the tube since it adheres so firmly to the finger. The commercial generally closes with the two friends talking again, one informing the other that he took the advice, bought the adhesive advertised, and now has no problems of slippage whatsoever. To demonstrate, he grasps his upper dentures between the tip of his thumb and the middle joint of his forefinger and tugs to show how firmly they remain in place. Because of the highly personal nature of denture wearing, the overly graphic portrayal of the slippage of the dentures as well as the manner in which the adhesive strength of the product is demonstrated tend to be, to a degree, repulsive. The same property of the product could be demonstrated in a far less graphic manner — actually in a story form that could prove more memorable and even bring about word-of-mouth advertising for the product. For example:

1. MS OF FATHER ADAM SEATED ON GROUND WITH LEGS UP AND ARMS AROUND THEM. HE IS LEANING AGAINST TRUNK OF TREE. TO HIS LEFT, EVE IS STANDING, VISIBLE ONLY FROM HIPS DOWN. SHE IS WEARING A BIKINI OF FIG LEAVES.	1. EVE: Adam?
1A. CU. EVE'S RIGHT HAND APPEARS HOLDING AN APPLE.	1A. EVE: Take a bite.
1B. CU. ADAM TURNS HEAD TO SEE APPLE.	1B. ADAM: You know I can't, Eve. EVE: Why not? ADAM: My chompers. Remember? They're the first set ever made.
1C. CU. EVE LIFTS APPLE OFF SCREEN.	1C. EVE: Adam. Bathroom closet. Second shelf. Blue and white package. Read the directions.
2. RIPPLE DISSOLVE TO MCU OF MIRRORED BATHROOM CLOSET FRAMED IN LEAVES AGAINST A WALL OF PALM FRONDS. ADAM IS SEEN IN MIRROR. HE EXTENDS RIGHT HAND AND OPENS DOOR, THEN REACHES FOR PACKAGE OF POLI-GRIP ON SECOND SHELF.	

3. RIPPLE DISSOLVE TO SAME SCENE AS IN FRAME 1. EVE'S HAND APPEARS AGAIN, HOLDING APPLE.	3. EVE: Try it now, Adam.
3A. MCU. ADAM TAKES APPLE, HOLDS IT TO MOUTH, BITES DEEPLY INTO IT. THUNDER AND LIGHTNING. EARTH SHAKES AND RUMBLES.	3A. SFX: THUNDERBOLT FOLLOWED BY RUMBLING THUNDER.
4. DISSOLVE TO MLS OF STONE ARCHWAY ENGRAVED WITH THE THE NAME: EDEN GARDENS. ADAM AND EVE WALK THROUGH IT. ADAM, FIRST, IS CARRYING A FOLDED SHEET OF BELONGINGS OVER HIS SHOULDER. EVE IS ALSO CARRYING ONE. THEY STOP.	4. EVE: I'm sorry, Adam. ADAM. It's okay. There's only one thing. EVE: What, Adam? ADAM: Did you remember to pack the Poli-Grip?

5.   CU OF PACKAGE.

In a treatment such as this there is a degree of entertainment and this is the principal reason people watch TV. The mere biting of an apple could have been the subject of a demonstration but, denture problems are very personal and seldom make welcome conversation. The use of humor, particularly in a fanciful story, removes the unpleasantness of the reality of dentures.

A commercial for Tucks, a product offering relief from hemorrhoidal discomfort, introduced a match slowly being ignited and bursting into flame to symbolize the discomfort of hemorrhoids and then showed a close-up of the product — a circular swatch of medicated cloth — being used to smother the flame. The symbolic demonstration was, like the Adam and Eve story, while not humorous, sufficiently off-subject to be acceptable. It is possible that the best solution for products that cause embarrassment when advertised on television is to convey the purpose and benefit of the product through a subject or a symbolic representation of use that functions, in a sense, as a mask for the product itself.

QUESTIONS, SUBJECTS FOR DISCUSSION

1. Should advertisers be permitted to advertise products of any kind on television?
2. Would a denial of this permission be considered a denial of freedom of speech?
3. Why is the employment of good taste in advertising of any kind advisable?
4. Why is it particularly advisable in television commercials?

PROJECT

Do a commercial for a product such as a hemorrhoidal ointment, a feminine hygiene product, a denture cleanser, or some similar type of product in such a way as to make it as close as possible to unobjectionable.

Chapter 38

ID's and 15-Second Spots

The ID (derived from "station identification") is a 10-second spot shown on the hour or half hour between programs. Ten seconds is precious little time in which to say anything about a product that might induce viewers to buy it. As a consequence, unless the ID is to be used solely to remind viewers of the product, the copywriter must use both the video and the audio parts of the commercial to exert maximum impact on the viewer. A visual device must be employed that is unusual and yet helps powerfully in conveying a desirable aspect of the product. Twenty words or fewer must sum up the principal benefit the product has to offer. For this purpose, the message should resort to any form of rhetoric that will be most likely to cause what is said to be remembered—a rhyme, a slogan, alliteration, or even a pun. In this respect, the ID is not unlike a billboard—its message should be clear but benefits from being clever (and, as a result, memorable) at the same time. For example, an ID for a coffee bought primarily for full and rich flavor such as Medaglia D'Oro:

VIDEO	AUDIO
1. CU OF CUP OF COFFEE ON TABLE. KNIFE COMES DOWN AND SLICES CUP (AND COFFEE IN IT) IN HALF.	1. ANNOUNCER (V.O.): If you like coffee so rich you can cut it with a knife . . .
2. CUT TO CU OF CAN OF MEDAGLIA D'ORO COFFEE.	2. ANNOUNCER (V.O.): . . . try Medaglia D'Oro.

Other ID's might employ other visuals. For example —

1. CU OF CUP OF COFFEE ON TABLE. HAND PUTS SPOON INTO COFFEE. SPOON STANDS UP.	1. ANNOUNCER (V.O.) If you like coffee so rich your spoon will stand up in it . . .
2. CUT TO CU OF CAN OF MEDAGLIA D'ORO.	2. ANNOUNCER (V.O.): . . . try Medaglia D'Oro.
1. CU OF CUP OF COFFEE. HAND STICKS FORK INTO IT AND LIFTS SEGMENT OF COFFEE OUT OF CUP.	1. ANNOUNCER (V.O.): If you like coffee so rich you can eat it with a fork . . .
2. CUT TO CU OF CAN OF MEDAGLIA D'ORO.	2. ANNOUNCER (V.O.): . . . try Medaglia D'Oro.

Nothing like this visual device is likely to have been used and, as a consequence, it registers vividly on the mind — at the same time that it brings to life what countless people have said for years in describing strong or rich coffee. It is interesting while achieving this and appears to be most readily attained by interpreting an "old saw" or a cliché in a curious and fanciful visual way.

Using another popular descriptive phrase, a memorable ID could be written for Hush Puppies — as follows:

VIDEO	AUDIO
1. CU OF MAN'S HANDS TYING LACES OF A HUSH PUPPY SHOE ON FOOT.	1. ANNOUNCER (V.O.): Hush Puppies are so pliable, so soft . . .
2. MLS OF A MAN WALKING DOG ON LEASH. DOG IS ON GROUND, MAN IS SIX TO EIGHT INCHES ABOVE IT.	2. ANNOUNCER (V.O.): . . . wearing them's like walking on air.

If an ID, as shown, conveys vividly a unique and primary advantage of a product, it provides an advertiser — because of its low cost — with the opportunity of high and effective frequency in use as compared with a 30-second and certainly a 60-second commercial. Because of the high cost of the 60-second commercial, the 30-second commercial was developed and, because of continued increases in the cost of television time, advertisers turned to 15-second commercials. In fifteen seconds as in ten seconds, there is time only for the briefest message about the product and, as in the ID, the audio and the video must be sufficiently unusual and arresting to register indelibly in the memory. Direct response advertisers who promote immediate purchase of whatever they advertise — record albums, magazine subscriptions — have found they must use 120 seconds of time in order for the offer to be effective, to cause the viewer to phone. This suggests, of course, that long commercials (like long print advertisements) are more productive than short ones and, by and large, they are. However, they must be in order to cover all the essential facts about the product advertised and to give directions for buying it. A direct response commercial could not possibly be effective if confined to 10 or 15 seconds. The ID as well as the 15-second commercial are necessarily going to have to be confined to products in general distribution. To compete successfully against other ID's or 15-second commercials, a short commercial must, beyond question, make a major impact on the memory — audibly as well as visibly.

QUESTIONS, SUBJECTS FOR DISCUSSION

1. What is essential in creating an ID that imposes maximum impact and memorability on the viewer?

2. Verbally, what rhetorical devices can be employed?

3. How should these be related to the product? In fact, in what way should the entire ID be related to the product?

4. In what way can a cliché contribute to the memorability of an ID?

PROJECT

Create three ID's or three 15-second commercials — one for a product, one for a service, and one for a public service announcement.

Chapter 39

Subliminal Advertising

In a book dedicated to the creation of advertising that is consciously accepted as more useful, more acceptable, and less irritating than most advertising currently printed and broadcast, the subject of subliminal advertising — which has stirred the curiosity and the concern of countless people — must be included.

Prior to 1956, subliminal advertising had never been mentioned in any of the advertising trade magazines, current or defunct, or in any of the newspaper advertising columns. The reason for this was that the term "subliminal advertising" as a form of marketing communication, had not yet been invented. It was invented in September of 1956 by a research specialist named James M. Vicary.

Actually, subliminal advertising was invented twice, first by Vicary and, then in 1972, by a Canadian university professor named Wilson Bryan Key. In the first of three books Key ultimately wrote on the subject entitled, respectively, *Subliminal Seduction, The Clam Plate Orgy*, and *Media Sexploitation*. Key's subliminal advertising differed from Vicary's in a number of respects. To begin what might be called the "subliminal era" in advertising, Vicary employed in a movie theater in Fort Lee, NJ a device known as a tachistoscope which he described as "a simple little electric eye, like the things that open and shut doors." This was attached to a projector that flashed the messages "Eat more popcorn" and "Drink more Coke" on a movie screen while a newsreel was being shown. They appeared for 1/3000th of a second, thus presumably registering on a subliminal level of awareness only. However, Vicary claimed Coke sales increased 18 percent and popcorn sales 58 percent.

Key's version of subliminal advertising was actually discovered rather than invented. In the first of his three books, Key reproduced, for example, a full-page advertisement for Gilbey's Gin which appeared in *Time* magazine. At the top of the advertisement was a headline which read *Break out the frosty bottle*. Below this and occupying most of the page was a photograph, reproduced in four colors, of a frosted bottle of Gilbey's Gin and, just to its right, a glass filled with a Tom Collins mix and five ice cubes. On the second, third and fourth cubes were three capital letters, not very well formed but there, nevertheless. The letters were S, E, and X.

Other advertisements appeared with the Gilbey ad in the center of Key's book. On page 7, Key referred to the advertisement and the letters S, E, and X on the ice cubes. He also called attention to what he considered the unseen sexual implants which he claimed were employed to provide "the subliminal promise" to anyone buying a bottle of Gilbey's of "a good old-fashioned sexual orgy." To quote him further:

> The melting ice on the bottle cap could symbolize seminal fluid—the origin of all human life. The green color suggests peace and tranquility after tensions have been released. Therefore, the scene is likely after orgasm, not before. This interpretation is reinforced by the less than fully extended penis. The melting ice on the frosty bottle, of course, could also suggest seminal fluid.

> . . . you might look between the reflection from the tonic glass and that of the bottle. The vertical opening between the reflection has subtle shadows on each side which could be interpreted as lips—vaginal lips, of course. At the top of the opening is a drop of water which could represent the clitoris.

The description, as given, suggests a Rorschach interpretation on the part of Key rather than the revelation of a hidden form of persuasion employed by the copywriter and the art director who created the advertisement. Regardless, Key's version of what he considers subliminal advertising differs from that of Vicary in another respect: it is presented with no test results proving the persuasive efficacy of the implants.

When Vicary announced what his form of subliminal advertising had accomplished in a movie theater in Fort Lee, New Jersey, the Copy Research Council — an assembly of research directors and top copywriters that met monthly in the Harvard Club in New York City to debate the reliability of various forms of advertising research — questioned the validity of both Vicary's claims and test findings and challenged him to repeat the test in the same theater and to have sales of Coca Cola and popcorn checked following the exposure of the audience to his flashed messages. Challenged by so authoritative a group, Vicary had no choice but to repeat the test. The same words were flashed at both the early showing and the late showing. No increase whatsoever in the sales of either Coca Cola or popcorn had occurred. Later, in an interview conducted by Advertising Age, Vicary admitted his "subliminal" advertising was a sheer "gimmick" he had created to attract attention and business to his failing research organization.

Nevertheless, belief in subliminal advertising did not abate and an attempt was made in the House of Representatives to pass legislation forbidding its use. Key's three books attained sales in the millions and he was heavily in demand as a lecturer on the subject, particularly at universities with advertising courses. A conspiracy among advertisers and advertising agencies to keep the subliminal use of advertising secret would be impossible. Articles on it and how best to employ it would appear regularly in the advertising trade press and books would be published on its use — and none has.

As for the authenticity of Key's discovery of sexual implants in advertising, on page 178 of *Subliminal Seduction*, he writes:

> Consider a Kent cigarette ad that was designed to appeal to the readers of *Cosmopolitan* (see page 24). Kent is a strong masculine name, suggesting a solid and distinguished Wasp heritage. Simply change the vowel form E to U, however, and Kent becomes the phonetic word symbol for the female genital.

If Key had been devoted to factual (not to mention spelling) accuracy, by phoning the manufacturer — Lorillard, Inc. — he could have learned that Kent was given its name because the president of the company at the time of its introduction was one Herbert Kent. As kindly as it can be put: QED.

QUESTIONS, SUBJECTS FOR DISCUSSION

1. What was James Vicary's method of projecting subliminal advertising messages?
2. Where did Vicary claim he had tested subliminal advertising?
3. What were the messages he projected?
4. What did he claim resulted following the projection of the messages?
5. What happened to Coke and popcorn sales when Vicary was challenged to repeat his subliminal messages under controlled conditions?

PROJECT

Obtain a dictionary definition of the term *subliminal* and do a paper explaining why advertising could not be subliminal and still accomplish its purpose.

Chapter 40

Advertising Ethics

Much has been said and written about advertising ethics. Most of what has been said and written finds advertising lacking in ethics. Before we condemn advertising, however, for lacking ethical principles, we should determine what we mean by "advertising." If we do we may conclude that finding advertising lacking in ethics is like finding typewriting lacking in precision. Both are activities practiced by human beings and, if one is lacking in ethics as the other is lacking in precision, the criticism must be directed at the practitioners rather than at the practice.

If we do this, we will find that most human activities cannot be totally free of unethical behavior. It would, in fact, be more realistic to state that all human activities in some way and to some degree can be found to be tainted with unethical behavior. The degree must be determined by the number of human beings engaged in the activity who condone and even defend unethical behavior by declaring that the end justifies the means; that if the end purpose of advertising is to induce individuals to buy a product, whatever is said to accomplish the end is justified. St. Jerome, in the third century, quoted this as a "line often adopted by strong men in controversy," so it is hardly a recent belief and reflects human behavior far before the time of St. Jerome. Not all advertising can be condemned as unethical but some must be since it is often the product of human beings who practice advertising with no regard for or thought of ethics. Considering the thousands of human beings employed in advertising, it is to be doubted that the practice of advertising will ever be totally ethical as it is to be doubted that any human activity, especially when individual gain is involved, will ever be totally ethical.

It would be far more gainful to examine and weigh the causes of ethical lack in the writing, publishing, or airing of advertising. When this is done, it will be found that the most likely cause is not simply the greed which exists in most human beings but the inability to satisfy that greed ethically – and this implies another lack: a lack of competence in the creation of advertising, in the manufacture of products and the development of services to be advertised. Products and services developed with incontrovertible benefits to those who purchase and use them require no deception or overstatement in the advertising created to promote their purchase and use. Competent development alone, however, cannot totally eliminate the possibility of "white lies" or one-sided presentation in advertising. When human beings promote themselves, they are seldom totally truthful. They are carefully selective in what they say of themselves. A truly competent presenter, a truly competent writer, can promote a product or a service and still present the product or the service the individual has to offer with full and total disclosure. Unfortunately, there are few truly competent presenters and few truly competent writers. As a consequence, it is strongly to be doubted if advertising and the people who practice it will ever be totally ethical.

While much of the criticism of advertising is as exaggerated as the advertising criticized, it is worth noting that few human practices benefit so much from a strict adherence to ethics as advertising. The closer the performance of the advertised product comes to duplicating what is claimed, the greater the assurance of satisfaction on the part of the customer and of that customer's continuing the purchase and use of the product. This requires on the part of the copywriter a respect for and dedication to accuracy in communicating. Of course, a respect for accuracy in communicating springs from a deep and abiding sense of ethics, and an undiminishing conviction that human beings must be able to believe the words they see and hear if human activity is to be fruitful.

Anyone contemplating a career in advertising should be aware that the advertising business exists only so long as it is acceptable to and tolerated by those to whom its messages are addressed. Because advertisers employ and make possible the earnings of the various manufacturers who bring advertising into being, too many of advertising's practitioners see the advertiser – the client – as the sole entity to be satisfied and the only goal-setter to whom they are responsible. Not only is this conclusion erroneous but, if believed, all too frequently results in the kind of advertising that is considered to be lacking in ethics, taste, or both, and so is actually of less value to the advertiser—or client—than it might have been. It must not be forgotten by creators of advertising that its cost is actually paid out of and is included in the price the public pays for the product or service advertised. The public, therefore, and only the public and its benefit, should be considered. As for the advertiser—the client—just as he or she must bear in mind the benefit of the public in the kind and type of product manufactured, so must he or she similarly bear in mind the goodwill and favor of the public in the kind and type of advertising published or aired.

Few human institutions come into being or remain without faults of some kind. In both taste and ethics, however, advertising has demonstrably improved over the years. It is the opportunity of anyone entering advertising, no matter what his or her position, to contribute to its further improvement. To do this one must always relate the advertising for which he or she is responsible to its audience, the public. It is here that ethical considerations must dominate and these must prevail for the benefit of all concerned, including the advertiser.

QUESTIONS, SUBJECTS FOR DISCUSSION

1. Why do you think a considerable number of people tend to think advertising is "unethical?" To check your thinking ask some of them.

2. Do you think any competitive human activity can be totally ethical? If so, state what kind or kinds.

3. What do you believe to be the major reason an advertiser might want to "overstate the case" for his product or service?

4. Whom should you primarily have in mind when you create **advertising**? And why?

5. In what ways can being ethical improve the contribution advertising makes to business?

PROJECT

Investigate the effect different cultures have on the ethics of the people who comprise them and what influence our ethical code reflects.

Chapter 41

Advertising
as of the Nineties

As this book goes to press, it has been estimated that advertising effectiveness has declined up to 60 percent from the degree of its effectiveness in stimulating reader and listener response in the 1980s.

As stated in the foregoing pages, it should be emphasized that the principles for attracting the attention of the target market, stimulating interest in what is being advertised, and bringing about acceptance and purchase of the brand featured, remain universally viable and dependable when employed as directed. In fact, those principles gain viability when adhered to and employed under current conditions. Essential to their successful use is an awareness and understanding of the nature of obstacles contributing to the reported decline. These are:

1. Major advertisers have decreased the proportion of the marketing dollar spent on advertising from 60 percent to 25 percent — while augmenting the proportion devoted to point of sale activity and dealer incentives from 40 percent to 75 percent. This has included a practice never before indulged in by major advertisers: payment to retailers for shelf space and shelf spacings. This space was formerly provided free so that retailers could benefit from the demand created by advertising. To counter this costly requirement, a number of advertisers instituted EDLP — or "every day low price." This merely emphasizes, however, the inevitability of having to sell on a price basis when there is too little or no brand demand.

2. Contributing also to the decline in advertising effectiveness has been corporate management's short-term "bottom line" thinking—which may be conducive to a favorable financial report but in no way enhances long-term product and company growth. Apparently gone is the policy of investment spending or backing a product with a substantial advertising expenditure to gain early volume and a major market share with a two- to five-year pay-out. In its place is the attempt to build "collective" market share through the constant introduction of new products, none of which employs a sufficient amount of advertising to build major demand. The consequent product proliferation also results in further reduction in brand preference through consumers experiencing the same difficulty of decision as the proverbial child standing before and looking into a bountifully stocked candy store window.

When Walter P. Chrysler introduced the Plymouth into the low-price automobile market, which was dominated by Ford and Chevrolet, his advertising agent, J. Stirling Getchell, was able in one year to make Plymouth equally acceptable with Ford and Chevrolet to low-price car buyers with the advertised challenge to *Look at All Three*. If Plymouth were being introduced today, the challenge—considering the number of sub-brands currently marketed by Ford and Chevrolet—would have to be to *Look at All Twenty-Seven*.

In few fields has the proliferation of brands been so voluminous as in ready-to-eat breakfast cereals. For many years there were three dominant brands—Kellogg's Corn Flakes, General Mills' Wheaties and General Foods Post Toasties. Today there are in excess of two hundred brands which occupy the entire shelf space on one side of a major supermarket aisle. There are more than two hundred and fifty soft drink brands and almost thirteen hundred brands and varieties of shampoo. Against this product inundation, the human mind is incapable of getting to know, remember, or develop preference for a particular brand. This prompts the assessment of still another factor in the reported decline in advertising effectiveness.

3. 15-second TV spots, quick cuts, and clutter—the last-named in print as well as broadcast advertising. The unnecessarily

and unjustified high cost of television time and television commercial production compelled TV advertisers first to switch
from 60-to 30-second spots and, as prices continued to mount,
to 15-second spots. At an allowable two words per second,
these restricted advertisers to 28-word messages. It also filled
station breaks with five or more commercials, taxing the memory's capacity to recall what it had looked at and heard. To
compound this, the use of quick cuts—or abbreviated and
chain-link video shots—has added mnemonic difficulty as
well as optical irritation.

In print ads, in order to project an original and distinctive
impression, advertisers ignore the findings of half a century of
reader research. For example, they print lengthy text in white
against a colored background or over an illustration, each
guaranteed to reduce the number of readers and the amount of
copy read. It is not surprising that up to 75 percent of adults
state that they find advertising—particularly television commercials—irritating, annoying, and "an insult to my intelligence."

Marketing in general and advertising in particular have going for
them—or against them—the attitude of the reader, listener, or
viewer. Only one of the major media that carry advertising—newspapers, magazines, radio, television, and billboards—is purchased
for its advertising. That medium is newspapers. Consumers buy
newspapers to see advertising they find useful and informative—
supermarket advertising, department and retail store advertising,
entertainment advertising, and classified advertising.

Confronted with the amount of advertising broadcast and published today, people inevitably develop attitudes toward kinds of
advertising. It is to management's cost and detriment that it fails to
bear this in mind. The latest advertising medium, for example, is
the telephone. Telemarketers tend to call between five and seven—
because at that time the entire family is available and usually at the
dinner table. One family member must exchange a knife or a fork or
a spoon for a telephone. Quite frequently the caller is not human but
a recorded message. Even a recorded message could apologize for
interrupting one's dinner, but it never does. Its sponsor is interested

in *selling*. It never occurs to him or to her that every day hundreds of thousands of consumers who are called by telemarketers not only can, by their attitude, contribute to the steep decline in advertising effectiveness but also adversely affect the public attitude toward advertising and its use.

Corporate management is slowly becoming aware of the importance of quality in consumer product acceptance. Entire industries that once employed hundreds of thousands of people no longer do so because they cannot compete on a quality basis with the Japanese, the Germans, or the Koreans. American advertising, once the wonder of the free enterprise system, is failing to move even quality merchandise. People no longer believe it. The element that caused numerous factories to fail may also put advertising out of business — lack of quality. It is the purpose of this book to prevent failure by making advertising — in all of its many forms — a quality product: not entertaining — simply informative and useful, and, as a consequence, interest-evoking, sales-inducing, and non-irritating.

Chapter 42

Career Routes

This chapter is strictly for students who have purchased this book. The major objective of taking a course in advertising at a university or elsewhere, is to obtain the foundation for a career in advertising — which requires getting a suitable job, either in an advertising agency or in the advertising department of a company.

There are other routes. If you plan a career in account service, becoming a salesperson with a major package goods advertiser (such as Procter & Gamble) can provide valuable background experience — or, if you intend to specialize in industrial advertising, it would be advisable to join a manufacturer of industrial products. Whatever you plan, the subsequent activity to education is working experience obtained through a job.

Getting a job for the first time is a project for which one has little experience or guidance. The usual university counsel is to prepare a résumé, but this is impractical for a number of reasons. First, even if you have been an A student, you have no practical experience to offer a prospective employer. Second, too many people send résumés, and even if printed and bound in leather, it will simply be one of many that arrive every morning on the personnel director's desk. Third, whatever your background, a résumé is of interest and value to a prospective employer — or personnel director — only after s/he has found reason for being interested in you and distinguishing you from the scores or hundreds of other individuals who'have prepared and sent résumés. Consequently, your first objective should be to learn what you can do to interest a prospective employer or personnel director and cause this individual to single you out from countless others who are looking for employment.

In this book you have discovered how to create interest in and induce purchase of products and services. When seeking a job, you are actually searching for someone to "buy" you. You are a "product" among many "products." Your challenge is to make yourself stand out; to create special interest to a sufficient degree to induce "purchase" of yourself.

The company you choose to work for is the "consumer" that you want to "buy" you. You must therefore present yourself as a "product" who can *benefit* the company more than any other "product" it can "buy." How can you make yourself unique and wanted? What can you offer that nobody else can or is even likely to offer? Try the following.

If you wish to interest an advertising agency in your capabilities, discover which companies are clients of the agency. To do this, go to a Free Public Library and ask for the red-bound *Standard Directory of Advertising Agencies*. This directory lists agencies by name alphabetically, the dollar amount of their billing, the advertisers that are clients, personnel, address, phone, and fax number.

If the agency you want to work for is too small to be listed in the *Standard Directory of Advertising Agencies*, learn who its clients are, the products or services it advertises, and media in which the advertising appears. Do this either by calling the agency or by asking the advertising manager of a local newspaper. Then do the following:

1. Read or listen to the advertising of as many of the agency's clients as you can find. If they advertise in trade papers, go back to the library and search for copies of the trade papers.

2. Using knowledge gained from this book re-do the advertising in ways to increase reader or listener interest and create layouts or story boards.

3. Visit retailers; ask to see the manager. Tell him or her you are doing a study of the influence of advertising on certain products. Ask the manager how well or poorly the product you are interested in learning about is selling, and what he or she thinks of the current advertising. Ask how the product or service is doing against competitive products or services. Find out if customers are satisfied or not. Make notes of your dis-

coveries. Present the advertising you have prepared and get the manager's opinion of it. Include any suggestions that will improve your work.

4. Prepare a presentation of your findings, and bind it. Write or call the *president* of the advertising agency. Tell the president you have done a research study of products the agency advertises and would like to show it to him/her or to someone s/he may designate. Arrange a suitable meeting time. At the meeting, explain your interest in working for the agency as demonstrated by the study, the written copy, and the layouts. Always write the president. If s/he cannot see you but is interested, whoever s/he asks to conduct the interview *will* see you and report back to the president. If you are hired, the president will remember you and will be interested in your progress with the company.

The chances that another person will do this are slim. Through this procedure you provide concrete evidence of your interest in working for the agency as well as a specific demonstration of how you think. If no job is currently available, ask if you may keep in touch and whom to call.

If you are interested in working for an advertiser, follow the same procedure. However, at the library ask for the red-bound *Standard Directory of Advertisers* which lists advertisers by product category or by manufactured product. The *Directory* also lists advertising expenditures, the media in which they advertise, and the percentage spent in each medium, as well as their address, company officers and titles, and the advertising agency or agencies that produce their advertising. When you have completed the research, prepare a presentation and advertising. Finally, write the president, explaining what you have done and what you have to show him.

Recommended Reading

This book is essentially a Baedeker, enabling a copywriter to arrive at the most effective kind of communication in and physical structure of the major forms of advertising, from print and broadcast messages to leaflets and envelope stuffers. The productivity of this kind of advertising depends largely on the copywriter's familiarity and knowledge of products, especially when asked to change a negative consumer response. This requires working in the particular field or reading books and magazines pertinent to it.

Advertising, as you will practice it, is closely allied with business. As a consequence, you should acquaint yourself daily with what is happening in the business world—in general as well as in specific areas in which the product or service being written about is distributed and sold. To keep current in what is happening in the world of business you should read *The New York Times*, both the daily and the Sunday edition. You should also read *The Wall Street Journal*, *Forbes*, and *Business Week*. If you cannot afford to buy or subscribe to them, read these publications at your local library, or make the acquaintance of the president of a local advertiser, find out if he or she subscribes to the *Journal*, *Forbes*, or *Business Week*, and ask if the secretary will save copies for you to pick up. You should, however, subscribe to *The New York Times*. You should also obtain and read the trade papers of the businesses you are advertising, and in addition, you can learn a great deal by calling on the retailers who sell the product you are advertising.

There are two major advertising trade publications—*Advertising Age* and *ADWEEK*. If you cannot afford to subscribe to either one, see the president of a local advertising agency and ask if copies could be saved for you to pick up.

If your aim as a copywriter is to create effective advertising, you must read books that contribute to the development of your writing skill—books written specifically to instruct you in writing as well as books (novels, poetry, essays) written by major writers. While reading, write out sentences or paragraphs that you find especially interesting or worth keeping; there is no better way to improve your creative ability. For example, in Virginia C. Bacon's *Good English* you find the following;

> Speech and thought are closely associated. If we lack a command of language, we are in danger of being incoherent not only to others but . . . to ourselves. Learning to use words effectively, framing exact, intelligible sentences, will improve our thinking and make it more precise.

In Mark Saxton's *Prepared for Rage* you will encounter this provocative observation:

> The world is gorged on facts and starving for reasons. The words that brought the world to its mortal agony are "what" and "when." The words that may save it are "how" and "why."

In Claude Bragdon's *The Beautiful Necessity*, about architecture, you will read this thoughtful reflection on elevators: "The elevator is more the cause than the effect of the skyscraper — it is the very piston of the machine."

There are certain combinations of words that open mental windows, that illuminate the mind. For example, from John Livingstone Lowes' *Convention and Revolt in Poetry:* "The cliche is merely the sometime novel that has been loved not wisely but too well." Or from Sir Arthur Eddington's *The Nature of the Physical World:*

> You remember the traveller (page 39) who went off to a distant star and returned absurdly young. He was a clock measuring two sides of a time-triangle. Need I defend my calling him a clock? We are all of us clocks whose faces tell the passing years.

Many such books are no longer in print or available for sale. However, many can be found at your local library, or the library can obtain them for you from other libraries.

In addition to the books quoted, a number of books either about the art of writing or written in a style that can help you improve your own writing include:

The Garment of Praise by Herbert Agar and Eleanor Carroll Chilton
Poetics by Aristotle
Counter-Statement by Kenneth Burke
The Poetry of Nonsense by Emile Cammaerts
On the Art of Writing by Sir Arthur Quiller-Couch
Greek Literary Criticism by J. B. Deniston
Discovering Poetry by Elizabeth Drew
The Opinions of Jerome Coignard by Anatole France
Art Epochs and Their Leaders by Oscar Hagen
A Writer's Notes on His Trade by C. E. Montague
Ion by Plato
Trivia by Logan Pearsall Smith
London River, Out of Soundings, Between the Lines, and *Old Junk*
    by H. M. Tomlinson
Variety by Paul Valery (translated by Malcolm Cowley)

Index

NOTES